Aelbert Cuyp

Stephen Reiss

AELBERT *Cuyp*

New York Graphic Society · Boston

International Standard Book Number 0-8212-0578-1

Library of Congress Catalog Number 73-91130

Published by New York Graphic Society, Ltd,
11 Beacon Street, Boston, Massachusetts 02108

Published in England
by A. Zwemmer Ltd, 26 Litchfield Street, London WC2

Printed in Great Britain

Contents

Colour Plates

Introduction

Facts concerning the life of Aelbert Cuyp are few. It is known that he was born in Dordrecht in October 1620, but between this date and his marriage in July 1658 the records are completely silent. Later he is mentioned fairly often: he moves house, takes on various honorary positions and, in time, becomes sufficiently respected to be appointed to the High Court of South Holland. But there is still no reference to him as a painter. This cannot be mere coincidence; it can only mean that in the eyes of his contemporaries – at least from 1658 onwards – he was not regarded primarily as an artist but as a man prominent in the affairs of his local community.

From a chronological study of his work, it becomes increasingly clear that his marriage may have been the signal for a definite change in his career. Perhaps, by this time, he felt he had fulfilled his ambition as a painter and wished to devote himself to other occupations. If so, it is possible his wife, Cornelia Bosman (1617–89), did little to dissuade him. She had a very strong religious background; not only was her father a clergyman but her maternal grandfather was one of the most influential theologians of the seventeenth century, a man notorious for his extreme Calvinism, Franciscus Gomarus (1561–1641). Her first husband, Jan van den Corput (1609–50), had been a naval officer and a member of one of Dordrecht's leading patrician families. It is perhaps significant that the year after her second marriage, Cuyp became deacon of the reformed church. Writing fifty years later, Houbraken remembered the painter as a devout Calvinist, and also mentions the fact that when he died (in November 1691) no pictures by other artists were found in his house. We have the strong impression that, whatever else she may have been, Cornelia was probably not a fervent patroness of the arts, and that Cuyp's own interest in painting flagged from about 1658 onwards.

His working career thus falls within the greatest period of Dutch painting, 1640–65. Both in terms of quantity and quality the production of pictures during these years reached an astonishingly high level. At the same time, the competition was so intense that several painters found it impossible to make a living solely by the sale of their work, and were obliged to take up another profession; others, like Cuyp and van der Cappelle, possessed sufficient private means to enable them to continue painting, untroubled by financial worries.

Any young artist, starting his career at about this time, must have found the choice of possible styles and subjects bewildering. Rembrandt, Hals and van Goyen were at the height of their powers, and a brilliant group of younger painters was just appearing on the scene: Jan Both, Philips Wouwerman, Nicolaes Berchem, Carel Dujardin, Paulus Potter, J. B. Weenix and Adam Pynacker. It was eventually with this group that Cuyp aligned himself, although his approach was essentially independent and he introduced many elements which cannot be found elsewhere.

Early period, 1639–48

His early development was affected by three main influences: Jacob Gerritsz Cuyp (1594–1651/2), Jan van Goyen (1596–1656) and Jan Both (*circa* 1614–52). In general terms, it could be said that Cuyp learnt form from his father, tone from van Goyen, and light from Both. Paradoxically, it was his father's influence that came last. This appears to have arisen from the fact that, being principally a portrait painter, Jacob Gerritsz at first employed his son mainly on providing the landscape backgrounds to his compositions; consequently it was only at a later date that Aelbert began to acquire a knowledge of representing figures and animals on a large scale.

It was probably in 1640 that he encountered the paintings of van Goyen. In the previous year his style was still completely unformed; this can be seen from two landscapes which are inscribed 1639 (R1 and 4), and as yet show no trace of external influence. Two years later, however, he was contributing van Goyenesque backgrounds to two portrait groups by Jacob Gerritsz with an assurance which suggests they were by no means his first attempts in the new style (R16 and 17). However, the handling is still hard and dry, and there is a dominant straw yellow tone characteristic of Cuyp's earliest work in the manner of The Hague painter. Later the handling becomes stronger and freer, and the lighting more concentrated. Perhaps the finest, and certainly the most ambitious, painting of this period is the *View of Dordrecht,* now unfortunately in two halves, divided between the museums of Leipzig and Los Angeles (R29 and 30). An early water-colour copy claims that it was painted in 1647, but essentially the style is that of the early 1640s.

Sometime during the mid-1640s, Cuyp's style changed fundamentally under the influence of Jan Both, who had just returned to his native Utrecht bringing with him a new system of composition which he had developed in Rome in the company of Claude Lorrain. This involved altering the direction of the light. Instead of placing it at right-angles to the line of vision, Both had moved it to a diagonal position at the back of the picture. Thus the artist more or less faced the sun, *contre-jour.* To intensify the

sense of luminosity and depth, much play was made on the use of elongated cast shadows. The compositional possibilities were enormous, as Cuyp was among the first to appreciate.

An indication that the date of his acquaintance with this method cannot have been later than 1645 is provided by the fact that his earliest *contre-jour* landscapes do not contain the exceptionally tall trees which were to become such a characteristic feature of Both's later work. Up to 1645 this particular feature was comparatively little in evidence. This is apparent from a *contre-jour* landscape by another Utrecht artist, Herman Saftleven (1609–85), which is dated 1644 (*see* p. 10). Moreover, the Cuyps had close connections with Utrecht; it was here that Jacob Gerritsz had studied and met Aertjen van Cooten, Aelbert's mother. That Aelbert was a frequent visitor to the town is shown by the many drawings he made of the neighbourhood.

It was basically through the use of *contre-jour,* and all that this implies in terms of light, that Cuyp's painting progressed from his early style to that of his maturity. Gradually the accessories (figures, animals, boats, etc.) became larger and the range of colour more ambitious. For a time, in fact, Cuyp went much further than any other painter of the seventeenth century in attempting to convey the full chromatic scale of sunset and sunrise (R44, 93 and 94). In such paintings he anticipates Turner and shows the essential originality of his approach. However, this particular phase was short-lived, being from Cuyp's point of view too exclusively impressionist.

JAN VAN GOYEN: *Windmill near a river*, dated 1642. National Gallery, London.

8

Far more difficult to decide is the exact manner in which Cuyp developed the means of representing large scale form. There exist a series of paintings (R51–66) which have strong iconographical connections with the work of Jacob Gerritsz Cuyp and appear stylistically to pre-date the influence of van Goyen and Jan Both, yet which include many features associated with the mid and late 1640s. It would be logical to attribute these paintings to the elder Cuyp, or to pupils other than Aelbert. But some have an authority which raises doubt. Inevitably, we are drawn to the conclusion that, between 1645 and 1650, the Cuyp studio was actively producing animal paintings quite independently of Jacob's main work as a portrait painter and Aelbert's personal exploration of pure landscape; but that nevertheless both the Cuyps made the occasional significant contribution.

Among the other major participants would undoubtedly have been Bastian Govertsz van der Leeuw (1624–80), whom Houbraken specifically records as an animal painter in the style of Jacob Cuyp, and who was registered as an apprentice in 1638.

Later period, 1649–62

While Cuyp's early development may be seen as a gradual progression towards greater breadth of handling, in his later work this process is put into reverse and his manner becomes steadily more formal, refined and decorative. In this respect his stylistic evolution is exactly parallel to that of the Dutch school generally.

To some extent, each phase can be associated with a particular atmospheric condition. Thus, around 1650, the atmosphere in several paintings seems sultry and oppressive; later on, the skies are consistently bright with light, fleecy clouds; and, finally, we sense that the air has the cool, crisp, yet slightly misty, character of late autumn. The colouring, even of the accessories, is carefully chosen to intensify these impressions.

A precise chronology is impossible, as the painter varied his style considerably according to the nature of his subject matter. An equestrian piece is likely to be more elegant than a painting of a passage-boat of about the same date. Nevertheless, we are able to establish a few landmarks by means of costume and the identification of the persons represented. For instance, it has been possible to identify the two boys in the equestrian piece in the Metropolitan Museum (R121); they are Michiel and Cornelis Pompe van Meerdervoort, the eldest grandchildren of a well-known Dordrecht statesman, Cornelis van Beveren (1591–1663). Their birthdates were 2 October 1638 and 16 December 1639, and their father died in 1639 just before the birth of his younger son; in this picture the boys are accompanied by their tutor, Caulier. As Michiel died on 20 November 1653, just after his fifteenth birthday, it is reasonable to assume that the picture was painted shortly before this date.

JAN BOTH: *Italian landscape with muleteers*. National Gallery, London.

Another commissioned picture which appears clearly to belong to the same date, perhaps a little earlier, is the *Avenue at Meerdervoort* in the Wallace Collection (R119); the combined presence of two ponies, two boys with a woman, and the family château at the side can hardly be mere coincidence. G. H. Veth records a long-standing tradition associating Cuyp with van Beveren (*Oud Holland* 1884, page 261), and it was doubtless he who commissioned both paintings and also a third: the equestrian piece in the Barber Institute (R122). Van Beveren had been knighted by Louis XIII in 1635 and this meant that he and his descendants were entitled to add a *fleur-de-lys* to their coat-of-arms. As this device is emblazoned on the saddle-cloth of the nearest horse in the Birmingham picture, it seems likely that the huntsmen are van Beveren's three sons: Willem (b. 1624), Jan (b. 1626) and Cornelis (b. *circa* 1632). It is not easy to assess their ages but a date between 1652 and 1655 seems likely, and this would be confirmed by their Polish style of dress which was especially fashionable in Holland during the early 1650s.

Costume considerations dictate that the *Negro Page* at Buckingham Palace (R113) must have been painted a few years earlier, and the elegant couple in the equestrian piece in the Washington Gallery (R124) anything up to ten years later. In both cases, horse brasses offer tenuous evidence which may help towards the identification of the persons represented. In the Buckingham Palace picture we again see the *fleur-de-lys,* which suggests van Beveren's eldest son, Willem, who was appointed Bailiff and Dyke-Reeve of the Lande van Strien in 1648; while the star, the Pompe family device, which hangs from the bridegroom's horse in the Washington picture, may signify that he is Cornelis Pompe, the younger of the two boys in the New York picture. Early in 1662 he married Alida van Beveren, a distant cousin. He looks older than twenty-two in this picture but x-ray examination shows that there has been considerable over-painting of the head.

Neither of these identifications is necessary, however, from the point of view of dating; costume is the decisive factor: *The Negro Page* is unlikely to be later than 1650, and the Washington picture cannot be earlier than 1660. It is essentially on the basis of these two dates, taken in combination with the three relating to the early 1650s, that the chronology of Cuyp's later period has been determined.

School Pictures, 1660–70

There is only one painting that closely compares in style with the Washington equestrian piece: the large landscape belonging to the Marquess of Bute (R140). In no other pictures do we find the same brittle, almost oriental, linear refinement. Inevitably we are drawn to the conclusion that these two works mark the final phase of his personal career as a painter, and that he was already by this time becoming less productive. Moreover, it seems clear that the period in question cannot be later than about 1660. Nevertheless, there still remain a considerable number of paintings of high quality for which no place can satisfactorily be found at an earlier date. Such pictures generally have one or more of three characteristics: a somewhat cluttered composition containing motifs drawn from various stages of Cuyp's career; an over-all pinkish tone lacking brilliance, or alternatively a too uniformly cold tonality; and an absence of a really strong, unifying sense of light.

This raises the question of the extent to which Cuyp operated a school or workshop. According to Houbraken, he gave lessons to Barent van Calraet (1649–1737) from the age of fifteen. As no other pupil is recorded it was previously assumed that none existed, but there is an increasing volume of evidence to suggest that there must in fact have been a relatively active and extensive workshop. No doubt Aelbert inherited his father's business and continued to operate it on roughly the same lines.

Among his principal followers was certainly Barent's elder brother, Abraham van Calraet (1642–1722). The theory has been put forward that this painter generally signed his pictures with the monogram A.C. While this may be true, we wonder to what extent the fact can have been recognised at the time. Strictly speaking Calraet's initials were not A.C. but A.v.C., and there is no evidence that the 'van' was ever dropped in any other circumstances. It seems inconceivable that Cuyp himself did not know that another painter was adopting his style as well as his initials; but, if he knew and presumably approved, is it not more likely that in fact the pictures were originating from his own studio and were being sold under *his* name and not that of Calraet? Houbraken unconsciously confirms this when, in his brief biography of Cuyp, he refers to two pictures by the artist, a cattle market and a riding school; such subjects are characteristic of the Calraets but completely untypical of Cuyp himself.

Possibly, then, the Cuyp workshop was producing two classes of picture: those inscribed with the artist's full signature which would imply a considerable contribution from the painter himself, and those merely signed with his initials which would mean the picture had been painted almost exclusively by a pupil or an assistant.

Cuyp in the eighteenth and nineteenth centuries

Not merely were these A.C. pictures considered genuine throughout the eighteenth and nineteenth centuries, they were also integrated into a theory as to how the artist's style had developed. Being highly finished in character it was supposed they were early works, a view which appeared to be supported by Houbraken's statement that Aelbert had started painting in a more precise manner than his father, Jacob Gerritsz Cuyp. Thus a catalogue of 1780 describes a picture as 'horses and figures preparing for the chase, *highly finished in his first manner*'.

As a result of this misunderstanding, Cuyp's genuine early landscapes – those in the style of van Goyen – were either overlooked or assigned to his father. Here again we frequently come

HERMAN SAFTLEVEN: *Mountainous landscape with peasants*, dated 1644. Present whereabouts unknown.

across references in eighteenth-century catalogues to landscapes by Old Cuyp or simply O. Cuyp and Bryan's *Dictionary of Painters*, published in 1816, even goes so far as to describe these as 'views in the neighbourhood of Dort, with figures and animals, which, though rather dry and hard in the pencilling, are not without merit for a natural and simple tone of colouring'.

From the earliest times, therefore, the whole structure of Cuyp's stylistic development was misinterpreted; paintings by his followers were thought to be his early work and his genuine early pictures were attributed to his father. However, the second mistake was only temporary. As the demand for Cuyp's paintings increased, any picture which could conceivably pass as his work was pressed into service.

It was particularly in England that he first became popular. A picture attributed to him (R144) fetched ninety guineas in 1759 and another (probably R103) two hundred and ninety guineas in 1774; although not quite at the top of the market, these were high prices at the time and implied a background of considerable interest in the artist. According to Benjamin West (as reported in Farington's *Diary* VIII page 178) it was the picture in the collection of the Marquess of Bute (R140) which originally led to the Cuyp vogue in this country: 'having been seen, pictures by Cuyp were eagerly sought for and many were introduced and sold to advantage'. This magnificent landscape was imported in about 1760 by Captain Baillie, and was engraved in 1764. Cuyp also became a special favourite with all the leading British landscape painters: first Wilson and Gainsborough, then Crome, Constable and Turner.

There were two periods of major speculation in Cuyp paintings during the nineteenth century, between 1800 and 1810, and between 1868 and 1875; the second period was inspired by the 140,000 francs paid in 1868 by Lord Hertford for the *Avenue at Meerdervoort* (R 119), at the time a record price for a landscape painting. By this date about 75 per cent of Cuyp's pictures had found their way to England and this near monopoly has in fact been one of the main reasons for the absence of literature on the painter. Having just acquired these pictures, English collectors promptly lost interest in them, under the successive influences of Ruskin, Berenson and Roger Fry.

Conclusion

Cuyp is no longer seen as a prolific, universal artist, 'a supreme craftsman in all styles' as Fromentin called him somewhat deprecatingly. Like most of the finest painters of his period, he was fundamentally a specialist. He has the remoteness of the true landscape painter; the human world did not greatly interest him, nor was he, on the whole, deeply affected by the work of other artists. Although he learnt much from van Goyen, Jan Both, and possibly Berchem and Pynacker, it is unlikely he had any

wish to become the collector of other people's paintings. This is one of the ways in which he differs from Vermeer, with whom he has otherwise a great deal in common. In a certain sense, he is one of the most abstract of artists; he seems completely absorbed by the formal and scientific aspects of nature, the fall of light, the effect of dampness in the atmosphere, the interplay of projection and recession, and the interpretation of aerial perspective. Ruskin was absolutely right when he said that Cuyp had no strong feelings about the puppies he painted, seeing 'nothing but the shine on the flaps of their ears'.

In the widest spectrum of Dutch painting, Cuyp can be described as the supreme master of the Utrecht school, the fulfilment not only of Both but of Bloemaert, a designer of pictures on a massive scale, even when the actual dimensions are small. In the past, he was known as the Dutch Claude, which is certainly not far from the truth, although his approach was in many ways more flexible and original than that of the French master. He

THOMAS GAINSBOROUGH: a free transcription of a cattle piece by Cuyp (R72). National Gallery of Ireland, Dublin.

freely attempted both classical and baroque methods of design and the sinewy strength of his line gives his paintings a unique position in the art of the seventeenth century. The individual components of his composition were fashioned with infinite care and each shape, whether the side of a cow or the hull of a boat, is given its maximum value as articulated form; and this also applies to each separate grouping of animals or river craft. This is one of the factors which especially enable us to distinguish his work from that of his followers.

Another quality that marks the difference between his painting and its imitation is the freedom and clarity of his brushwork. His touch is always *alla-prima*, crisp and fresh; any appearance of tiredness or worry in the handling of the pigment denotes, if not the work of a follower, then poor condition or heavy restoration. It must be remembered that, in the past, Cuyp was always honoured first and foremost as a colourist. As Bryan wrote in his *Dictionary* in 1816: 'Tuned to the harmony of colour, like the ear of a musician to sound, his eye appears to have been incapable of a discordant tone.'

Like all the great masters of the seventeenth century, he was principally a painter of light. As Constable said: 'Chiaroscuro is by no means confined to dark pictures: the works of Cuyp, though generally light, are full of it. It may be defined as that power which creates space'. And also Fromentin: 'He had that uncommon power of first imagining an atmosphere and then making of it not only the vanishing, fluid and breathable element, but also the law, and, so to speak, the ruling principle of his pictures'.

Over the past three centuries, the number of pictures attributed to Cuyp has steadily increased, and more than two thousand candidates scattered throughout the world compete for consideration. To examine all their claims in detail would be impossible. The most that can be attempted is to establish a simple canon of works whose authenticity is least open to doubt, and on the basis of which further attributions can safely be added. Cuyp is here pictured as almost exclusively a landscape artist. The theory that he also painted conventional portraits, church interiors, battle scenes, genre, poultry and fruit has never been established. Nevertheless, comparative tables are provided which it is hoped will assist in tracing the present whereabouts of pictures attributed to Cuyp in the earlier catalogues of John Smith and Hofstede de Groot.

Reference to the provenance of pictures has been deliberately restricted to a minimum. With one exception (R121), no painting has a history which can be traced to a date earlier than 1745; by this time, as has been shown, a completely false interpretation of the painter had already developed. It follows that the pedigree of pictures, however long and impressive, can only tend to deceive. This is reinforced by the analysis of the famous Slinge-land collection on page 212. Although formed in Dordrecht during the middle years of the eighteenth century, less than half the 38 pictures sold in 1785 would now be considered genuine.

What is basically lacking in the case of Cuyp is anything approaching a consensus of expert opinion. No reliable views can be quoted. The most, therefore, that any writer can hope to offer at this stage is a preliminary contribution towards a more solid basis of appreciation and study.

1 Farm scene (*Lady Teresa Agnew*) R7

II River scene, two men conversing (*Dordrecht Museum*) R13

III Detail: River scene with angler (*National Gallery, London*) R19

IV Dordrecht in a thunderstorm (*Collection E. G. Bührle*) R27

V Dordrecht: Sunrise (*copyright The Frick Collection, New York*) R94

VI Muleteers in a hilly landscape (*Cleveland Museum of Art*) R46

VII River scene with cattle and anglers (*National Gallery, London*) R88

VIII The Maas at Dordrecht (*National Gallery of Art, Washington*) R104

IX Detail: Dordrecht at dawn (*Private Collection*) R110

X Cavaliers watering their steeds (*Rijksmuseum, Amsterdam*) R139

XI Detail: River landscape with horseman and peasants (*Marquess of Bute*) R140

XII Lady and gentleman on horseback (*National Gallery of Art, Washington*) R124

Style of 1639

1 Landscape with cattle
panel 14½ × 18½in./37 × 47cm., inscribed *A. cuyp fecit* **1639**
Besançon Museum
first recorded 1840
painted in 1639; reference HdG362

Although probably painted when the artist was only eighteen,
this and the three succeeding pictures show little evidence of
exceptional precocity. Paulus Potter, for example, was
considerably more accomplished by the time he was eighteen.
Except in the drawing of the cattle, they appear to owe
nothing to Jacob Gerritsz Cuyp. On the other hand, it may be
possible to trace a slight affinity with the work of the Gorcum
painters, the Camphuysens and the early Aert van der Neer,
or with that of L. Bernaerts of Middelburg. This particular
painting is in poor condition. One notes the inward looking
figure, a device which frequently recurs in Cuyp's work and
symbolizes the difference between his approach and that of
his father, whose figures and animals invariably face towards
the spectator.

2 Landscape with cattle

panel 18×21½in./45×54·5cm., inscribed *A. cuyp fecit*
Private collection, London
first recorded collection Earl of Stradbroke *circa* 1920
painted *circa* 1639

In far better condition than the previous work but in identical
style, this picture shows the meticulous attention to detail which
is perhaps the strongest feature of Cuyp's earliest manner. The
colouring is cool and subdued, with a dominance of grey and
pale green.

The cow in the immediate foreground has been directly
transcribed from a drawing by J. G. Cuyp which was one of
several engraved by R. Persyn and published in 1641 by
Nicolaes Visscher under the title *Diversa Animalia Quadrupedia
ad vivum delineata a Iacobo Cupio*. The engraving (number 6 in
the series) is reproduced in reverse.

3 Avenue near Dordrecht
panel 17×21in./43×53cm., inscribed *A. cuyp fecit*
Present whereabouts unknown
first recorded E. Heimgartner, Geneva 1926
painted *circa* 1639

Another painting in identical style to the two preceding works
and possibly even a little earlier. Such pictures could easily be
overlooked but for the naïve originality of their method of
composition.

4 Quayside, Dordrecht
panel $23\frac{1}{2} \times 29\frac{1}{2}$in./58·5 × 73·5cm., inscribed *A. cuyp 1639*
Present whereabouts unknown
first recorded Brunner Gallery, Paris 1919
painted in 1639

Perhaps marginally later than the three preceding pictures but
still very similar; note again the inward looking figure with the
basket. A possible influence here is Simon de Vlieger
(*circa* 1600-53), one of the major catalystic forces of the 1640s.

5 Orpheus
panel 16 × 21in./39 × 53cm.
Gemälde-Galerie, Dessau
first recorded 1877
painted *circa* 1640; reference HdG 18

As painters of animals, it is natural that the Cuyps should
have been drawn to the Orpheus theme. In this case, Aelbert
has made much use of material provided by his father, not only
the two drawings from *Diversa Animalia* reproduced on the left
(numbers 7 and 8), but also a sketch of tigers which was with
the firm of J. Vlug, Brussels, in 1947. In the distance can be
seen the Merwede tower, a familiar landmark about a mile
east of Dordrecht.

6 Baptism of the Eunuch
panel 41½ × 58in./104 × 145cm., inscribed *A. cuyp*
J. de Menil, Houston, Texas
first recorded Amsterdam sale 1827
painted 1639/40; reference HdG 11a

Considerably larger than the preceding works, the next two
paintings are handled with much greater freedom and
confidence. This particular painting suggests a Utrecht
influence, perhaps that of Gysbert de Hondecoeter (1604–53).
Drawings show that Cuyp must have spent some time in and
around Utrecht at about this date. The handling of the subject
appears to be based on a well-known etching by van Vliet after
a supposed lost original by Rembrandt.

7 Farm scene
Canvas 42 × 62in./105 × 155cm., inscribed *A. cuyp*
Lady Teresa Agnew, Melbury Park
first recorded Hendrik Verschuuring sale 1770
painted 1639-40; reference HdG 228b and 699
reproduced in colour, plate I

The finest surviving painting of Cuyp's first, pre-van
Goyenesque period, although still curiously lacking the specific
qualities for which the artist is finally most valued. In its
somewhat unselective realism, it would be almost more at
home in 1840 than 1640.

The influence of van Goyen

8 Landscape with two windmills
panel hexagonal 16½in. × 21½in./41 × 54cm., inscribed *A. cuyp*
Art trade 1969
first recorded Wynn Ellis sale 1876 (?)
painted *circa* 1640; reference HdG 715

The influence of van Goyen is mainly detected by Cuyp's use
of The Hague painter's characteristic broken brush technique.
In other respects, the changes are hardly perceptible. In a
sense, van Goyen simply gave added impetus to a course to
which Cuyp was already essentially committed.

36

9 Landscape with shepherds
panel $15\frac{1}{2} \times 21\frac{1}{2}$in./$39\cdot5 \times 54\cdot5$cm., inscribed *A. cuyp*
Private collection, London
first recorded collection Pfungst 1903
painted *circa* 1640; reference HdG 691

One of the sketchiest of Cuyp's van Goyenesque paintings;
in fact, there is hardly sufficient paint for comfort. The
extraordinarily long shepherd's crook shows how little Cuyp
was concerned with realistic proportions.

10 Meadow beside a river
panel $17\frac{1}{2} \times 29\frac{1}{2}$ in./$43\cdot5 \times 74$cm., inscribed *A. cuyp*
Museum Boymans-van Beuningen, Rotterdam
first recorded *circa* 1930 London art trade
painted *circa* 1640

Also rather summary in its handling (see R9) but the sky is fine.
A second version, 11×16 in./27×41 cm., was in the Ridder
sale in 1924 (HdG 219 and 687). This is said to bear the
initials A.v.S. which suggests it may be a copy by Abraham
van Strij. It is here reproduced from an old photograph.

11 Wooded landscape near Utrecht
panel 19½ × 29in./49 × 74cm., inscribed *A. cuyp fecit 16...*
Residenz-Galerie, Salzburg
first recorded collection Count Czernin 1863
painted 1640/41, reference HdG 712

J. G. van Gelder and Ingrid Jost have shown how this picture
is a composite construction based on two quite independent
drawings by the artist (cf. *Miscellanea IQ van Regteren Altena*
1669 pp. 100–103). It is also interesting to note how little
Cuyp's handling of cattle has changed since he painted R2.

12 Road through the dunes
panel 19½ × 29in./49 × 73cm., twice inscribed *A. cuyp*
Destroyed by fire 1945 (Kaiser Friedrich, Berlin)
first recorded 1873
painted 1640/41; reference HdG 683

This and two other paintings attributed to Cuyp's
van Goyenesque period were lost in a fire in Berlin in 1945. Of
the three, this appears to have been the most characteristic of
the artist.

Reproduced from a print of poor quality. The lost panel was,
in fact, slightly larger than the painting opposite.

13 River scene, two men conversing
panel 16½ × 26in./42 × 65cm., inscribed *A. cuyp*
Dordrecht Museum
first recorded with Sedelmeyer 1889
painted *circa* 1641; reference HdG 688
reproduced in colour, plate II

One of the finest of what may be described as Cuyp's primitive
van Goyenesque paintings. Note again the figure with the
basket, though not in this case used as a compositional device
to draw the eye inwards towards the centre of the picture. The
success of the work lies in the subtle distribution of light and
shade, and especially in the articulation of the four vertical
shapes.

14 Herdsman and two cows
panel $17\frac{1}{2} \times 29\frac{1}{2}$in./44×74cm., inscribed *A. cuyp*
Present whereabouts unknown
first recorded London art trade *circa* 1930
painted *circa* 1641

Rather coarsely painted by comparison with R13. The inward
looking figure now leans on a stick and no longer carries a
basket.

15 Landscape with shepherds, cattle and goats
panel 16×23½in./40×59cm., inscribed *A. cuyp*
Dulwich College Picture Gallery, London
first recorded Desenfans sale 1802
painted *circa* 1641; reference HdG 239 and 697

Painted with a richer impasto than most of Cuyp's early works
and in an exceptionally light key. The figures are also unusual.
Use is still being made of drawings by J. G. Cuyp (number 13
in *Diversa Animalia*).

16 Family portrait group
canvas 62×100in./155×249cm., inscribed *cuyp fecit 1641*
Israel Museum, Jerusalem
first recorded collection Baron E. Rothschild 1892
jointly painted in 1641 by J. G. and A. Cuyp

It is intriguing that the only two paintings acknowledged as
a collaboration between the two Cuyps (Jacob painting the
portraits and Aelbert the landscape backgrounds) should both
be dated 1641. R17 is obviously the more successful. With so
many portraits to encompass, this picture inevitably
appears somewhat stilted but is of immense interest as a
stylistic record. Aelbert probably reverted to a fringe of plants
in the foreground from necessity rather than choice.

44

17 Portrait group near Rhenen
canvas 42×58in./107×147cm., inscribed *J. G. cuyp fecit 1641*
Paula de Koenigsberg, Buenos Aires
first recorded J. Jelfs sale 1773
jointly painted in 1641 by J. G. and A. Cuyp; reference
HdG 69a

In this case not only the figures but also the sheep are the work
of Jacob Gerritsz. The view of Rhenen, which Aelbert painted
as the background, has been directly transcribed from a drawing
now in the Teyler Museum at Haarlem (reproduced on the
right).

18 River landscape with bridge
panel 16 × 22in./40 × 55cm., inscribed *A. cuyp*
Städelsches Kunstinstitut, Frankfurt
first recorded in a Munich exhibition 1869
painted *circa* 1642; reference HdG 689

Faultlessly composed and coloured with great subtlety, this
and R19 are without doubt the masterpieces of Cuyp's second,
or middle, van Goyenesque period. Like so many of Cuyp's
early paintings they are based on drawings (in this case Hind 9
in the British Museum).

19 River scene with angler
panel $14 \times 20\frac{1}{2}$in./37×52cm., inscribed *A. cuyp*
National Gallery, London (by courtesy of the Trustees)
first recorded collection Charles Bredel 1851
painted *circa* 1642; reference HdG 638, 667 and 677
reproduced in colour, plate III

Cuyp never came closer to the plein-air technique of the
Impressionists, nor painted a picture more daring in its
simplicity. Its many exceptional qualities make it difficult to
date with confidence, and B. Haak (*Antiek* May 1973, p. 715)
has argued that it would seem at least a year or two later than,
for instance, R22.

20 Landscape with white horse
panel 16½ × 22in./42 × 55cm., inscribed *A. cuyp*
London sale, 28 June 1974
first recorded Amsterdam sale 1904
painted *circa* 1642; reference HdG 703

Handled in a more perfunctory manner than the two preceding
paintings, this and R21 suggest an attempt – not entirely suited
to Cuyp's temperament – to emulate van Goyen's swift
calligraphic technique. The white horse has already been seen
in the *Orpheus* (R5).

21 River scene with windmill

panel 17×26in./42×64cm., inscribed *A. cuyp*
A. Laan, Bloemendael
first recorded collection Bishop Godd, Leeds, 1933
painted *circa* 1642

Comparison with R4 shows the extent to which the painter
has progressed in a matter of two or three years. A drawing
(Van Beuningen collection, Rotterdam) is again the basis of
the picture.

A somewhat similar picture (HdG 635 and 662) has recently
appeared in the art market. A certain lack of subtlety in the
composition — though the effect of light is fine — suggests that
it was one of the very earliest of Cuyp's paintings in the manner
of van Goyen. It should also be compared with R13.

22 Rietdijkspoort, Dordrecht

panel 7½ × 13in./18 × 32cm., inscribed *A. cuyp*
Trustees Assheton-Bennett Collection
first recorded J. van der Linden van Slingeland sale 1785
painted *circa* 1642; reference HdG 650c

Although it clearly represents the Rietdijkspoort, this small
sketch introduces an imaginary bank beyond and to the right
of the buildings. The same view was again used some years
later in a picture which may be the work of a pupil
(ex collection Lord Claud Hamilton) and of which there is a
copy in the Museum of Fine Arts, Budapest.

23 Horesman and two beggar-boys
panel $9\frac{1}{2} \times 18$in./24×45cm.
Private collection, England
first recorded Tronchin sale 1780
painted *circa* 1644, reference HdG 473 and 473a

A slight sketch of this nature is difficult to date with accuracy,
and this particular work could well have been painted a year
or two later than 1644. The walled town is thought to be
Wageningen (see R25). An associated drawing is in the British
Museum. The same view also appears in a small sketch in the
Corcoran Gallery (HdG 701).

24 View of Amersfoort
canvas 39 × 55in./97 × 136·5cm., inscribed *A. cuyp*
Städtisches Museum, Wuppertal
first recorded collection Bayer 1909
painted *circa* 1644

This and the succeeding nine pictures may be classified as late
van Goyenesque. Darker in tone than their predecessors,
they generally have a panoramic character and represent
distant views of towns. This example is in poor condition.
There is a related drawing in Edinburgh.

25 Distant view of a town (?Wageningen)
panel 19 × 27½in./48 × 70cm., incribed *A. cuyp*
Old Town Hall, Cape Town
first recorded Max Michaelis collection 1913
painted *circa* 1644

Cuyp's authorship of this painting is proposed with some
reservation. It is thinly painted and has several features in
common with R59 and R69; however, the composition and
draughtsmanship are convincing. The view of the town is
identical with that appearing in R23.

26 View of a town on a river (?Vianen)
panel 15 × 21in./37 × 52cm., inscribed *A. cuyp*
Private collection, England
first recorded Grafton Gallery exhibition 1911
painted *circa* 1644

This and the succeeding work show Cuyp attempting to extend
the range of his art by introducing dramatic effects, possibly
under the influence of Benjamin Cuyp (1612–52). Vianen is
just south of Utrecht and in a part of the country much
frequented by the artist.

27 Dordrecht in a thunderstorm
panel 30 × 42in./75 × 105cm., inscribed *A. cuyp*
Collection E. G. Bührle, Zurich
first recorded at Ham House eighteenth century
painted *circa* 1644; reference HdG 708
reproduced in colour, plate IV

Although there are certain affinities in the handling of the
cattle between this work and the Melbury Park landscape (R7),
de Groot can hardly be correct in describing it as '*very* early'.
The picture much impressed Constable: 'a truly sublime Cuyp,
a tempest, still mild, and tranquil . . . I wish I had seen it
before I sent my "Salisbury" away.'

Simon de Vlieger (*circa* 1600–53): The Oostpoort, Rotterdam
Kunsthalle, Hamburg
panel 10 × 15in./41 × 62·5cm.

De Vlieger was one of the most ubiquitous and versatile
painters of the seventeenth century, and it seems more than
likely that Cuyp knew his work and perhaps received some
direct encouragement from him. This picture was painted in
about 1640.

28 River scene at Dordrecht, morning
canvas 39×55in./97×137cm., inscribed *A. cuyp*
*Toledo Museum of Art, Toledo, Ohio (Gift of Edward
Drummond Libbey)*
first recorded Amsterdam sale 1763
painted *circa* 1644; reference HdG 648a

The tower is apparently that of the Groothoofdspoort at
Dordrecht, as seen from the south-west. This is one of a group
of pictures in which the signature appears on a plank in the
water; see also R32, 33, 34 and 63.

29 View of Dordrecht (left half)
panel 19½×30in./49·5×76cm.
*County Museum of Art, Los Angeles (Adele S. Browning
Memorial Collection)*
first recorded J. A. Brentano sale 1822
painted *circa* 1644; reference HdG 249

That this and R30 originally formed one picture was recognised
as a result of a watercolour copy by Aert Schouman. The
implications of this discovery are discussed on the two following
pages.

30 View of Dordrecht (right half)
panel 20 × 34in./50·5 × 86cm.
Museum der bildenden Künste, Leipzig
first recorded London sale 1892
painted *circa* 1644; reference HdG 634

Without realising that they were only looking at half a picture,
both de Groot and Dr Bode considered this to be the finest
painting of Cuyp's early period. The sailing boats are closely
comparable with those appearing in R13.

This drawing (152×294mm.) by the Dordrecht artist Aert Schouman (1710–92) formerly belonged to Dr. L. Fröhlich Bume and was sold at Sotheby's in March 1973. It carries the inscription: *A cuyp.Pinx.1647. | de Stadt DORDRECHT. | A. Schouman del. 1759.* On what evidence Schouman asserts that the original was painted in 1647 is not known. In their *Doorzagen op Aelbert Cuyp* in the *Nederlands Kunsthistorisch Jaarboek 1972* pp. 23–39, J. G. van Gelder and Ingrid Jost have shown on topographical grounds that both the painting and the drawing for it (collection E. Sexton) would be consistent with a date not later than the early months of 1647. According to the chronology here proposed the picture can hardly have been painted later than 1645; the handling is still essentially van Goyenesque and there is as yet no hint of *contre-jour*. Possibly Schouman was reading an indistinct inscription which has since disappeared or he deduced the date on similar grounds to the van Gelders.

View of Dordrecht
A reconstruction based on R29 and R30

Although the drawing opposite is by no means accurate in
every detail, it is probably not too far wrong in its
representation of the over-all proportions. If so, it is evident
that a large section of the sky was discarded at the time the
panel was sawn in half, and that the original picture must have
measured about 33×66in. (82×164cm.). Presumably this
additional act of vandalism was considered necessary to provide
the two new panels with reasonably balanced proportions.

31 River scene with small tower
panel 19 × 29in./47 × 72cm., inscribed *A. cuyp*
Private collection, London
first recorded London sale 22 March 1966
painted *circa* 1644

One of about half a dozen pictures of undoubted authenticity
which have recently come to light and whose previous history
is completely unrecorded.

32 Fishing boat at anchor
panel 19 × 40½in./47 × 101cm., inscribed *A. cuyp*
Private collection, London
first recorded J. van der Marck sale 1773
painted *circa* 1644; reference HdG 648b and 649

Very similar in style to the Los Angeles-Leipzig *View of Dordrecht* (R29/30) and one of the classic paintings of Cuyp's early period. The sailing boat at anchor reappears in three paintings of a later date: R94, 95 and 104.

33 A river estuary
panel 18 × 29in./45 × 72cm., inscribed *A. cuyp*
John G. Johnson Collection, Philadelphia
first recorded Van Saceghem sale 1851
painted *circa* 1644; reference HdG 661a

The name of J. van Diest (*circa* 1631–*circa* 1673) has sometimes
been put forward in relation to this picture but brushwork,
colouring and the handling of the figures are entirely
characteristic of Cuyp. The painter's name again appears on
a plank in the water (see R28, 32, 34 and 63).

34 Moonlit river scene with windmill
panel 30½ × 42in./76·5 × 105cm., inscribed *A. cuyp*
Stadtmuseum, Cologne
first recorded London sale 1802
painted *circa* 1644; reference HdG 720, 727

Although Houbraken speaks of several moonlight scenes by
Cuyp, this is the only one which can be accepted with
confidence (for two other possible candidates see R75 and R77).
It is among the artist's finest works and the date may well be
later than here suggested. It was engraved by S. W.
Reynolds in about 1800.

Contre-jour and early Italianate

35 Peasants and cattle in a hilly landscape
panel 26×35in./65×87·5cm., inscribed *A. cuyp*
London sale, 28 May 1937
first recorded Hannah Entwistle sale 1908
painted *circa* 1645; reference HdG 412

There is no obvious indication as to which is the earliest of
Cuyp's *contre-jour* paintings. He was at this stage in his
career able to switch from one style to another without
betraying any signs of incompetence; however, R35 and 36
are certainly among the more conventional of his efforts in
the new manner.

36 Shepherds and shepherdess in rocky landscape
panel 17 × 24½in./43 × 62cm., inscribed *A. cuyp*
Private collection, Switzerland
first recorded London sale 1957 (Lord Falmouth)
painted *circa* 1645

Another of the pictures (see R31) which remained unrecognized
in this country for perhaps two centuries, having been bought
originally for their subject rather than their name.

37 Two horsemen in a hilly landscape
panel 26½ × 36in./66 × 90cm., inscribed *A. cuyp*
Rijksmuseum, Amsterdam
first recorded collection A. de Lelie 1810
painted *circa* 1645; reference HdG 406

Perhaps the best known and most characteristic of Cuyp's
early *contre-jour* paintings.

38 Shepherds and shepherdess near a well
panel 30×42in./75×110cm., inscribed *A. cuyp*
Private collection, U.S.A.
first recorded London sale 1938
painted *circa* 1645

One sees especially from this picture that the influence of
Jan Both was largely that of a catalyst. The approach is entirely
personal. The picture also demonstrates the two sides of
Cuyp's personality, in this case his striving after refinement
and elegance of handling. There are certain similarities
with R24.

39 Travellers, herdsmen and cattle
panel 21 × 29½in./52·5 × 74cm., inscribed *A. cuyp*
Stitching Nederlands Kunstbezit
first recorded J. van der Linden van Slingeland sale 1785
painted *circa* 1646; reference HdG 389 and 398

The colouring of Cuyp's early *contre-jour* paintings tends
towards apricot and olive-green as distinct from the grey, brown
and straw yellow of his van Goyenesque phase.

40 Merwede tower, evening
panel 21×33in./53×83cm., inscribed *A. cuyp*
Musée Fabre, Montpellier
first recorded J. F. Tuffen sale 1818
painted *circa* 1646; reference HdG 172

Cuyp was among the first to apply *contre-jour* to the painting
of domestic landscape; others to do so include Paulus Potter
and Simon de Vlieger. This picture, one of Cuyp's early
masterpieces, already contains strong elements foreshadowing
his mature style. The trawler at anchor is repeated from R28.

41 Horsemen dismounted near Rhenen
panel 27 × 36in./67·5 × 90·5cm., inscribed *A. cuyp*
Kruppsche Gemäldesammlung, Essen
first recorded D. vis Blokhuyzen sale 1870
painted *circa* 1645; reference HdG 75

A little-known picture which helps to complete this small
group of early *contre-jour* paintings. The view of Rhenen
is based on drawings (Teyler Museum and Berlin) which also
did service for R17 and 42.

42 Herdsmen and cattle near Rhenen
panel 19 × 29in./47·5 × 72·5cm. inscribed *A. cuyp*
Dulwich College Picture Gallery, London
first recorded collection Desenfans *circa* 1810
painted *circa* 1646; reference HdG 694

Cuyp's brush technique, for example in the handling of the
trees, is at this stage of his career very close to that of Jacob
Gerritsz Cuyp. This led the present writer mistakenly to
attribute the picture to the elder Cuyp (*Burlington Magazine,*
February 1953).

43 Milking scene near a river
panel 18½×29in./47×72cm., inscribed *A. cuyp*
Present whereabouts unknown
first recorded collection Earl of Lichfield *circa* 1780
painted *circa* 1646; reference HdG 374

Cuyp never went further in attempting a completely natural,
almost photographic, handling of composition and colour.
The picture, which was engraved by Thomas Morris in about
1780, was much copied not only in the seventeenth century but
also later. It represents one of the most critically important
landmarks in the evolution of the painter's style and deserves
to be better known. See also note to R57.

44 Mountainous landscape with herdsmen and cattle
canvas 39×57in./99×142cm., inscribed *A. cuyp*
Dulwich College Picture Gallery, London
first recorded Michael Bryan sale 1798
painted *circa* 1646; reference HdG 237e and 330

Another of a small group of paintings in which Cuyp explores
atmospheric colouring. Hazlitt described it as 'woven of
ethereal hues' and as 'the finest Cuyp perhaps in the world',
but Ruskin complained that 'there is no such thing as a
serene sunset sky with its purple and rose in BELTS around
the sun'. There is, in fact, some dispute as to whether morning
or evening is represented. Compare the back-turned figure
with that in R24.

This and R43 are among the earliest pictures which can be
connected with Cuyp's etchings. Only eight of these are known;
all are small, hastily drawn and depict cattle. Iconographically,
they appear to date from the late 1640s. The D numbers given
here and subsequently refer to Dutuit, *Manuel de l'Amateur
d'Estampes, 1881–88.*

Etching by A. Cuyp reproduced in reverse (D4).

45 Two shepherds in a hilly landscape
panel 24×32in./60×80cm., inscribed *A. cuyp*
Mrs Julian Salmond, Malmesbury
first recorded Jacob Spex sale 1777
painted *circa* 1646; reference HdG 230a

It is a mystery how and when this picture came into the
possession of the Cowper family, from whom the present owner
is descended, and why none of the visitors to Panshanger (for
instance Dr Waagen) seems to have noticed it. Although not in
pristine condition and a little unusual in that it is a work of
the transition between the painter's early and mature styles,
it is wholly typical in its colouring – clear vermilion against
yellow browns and pale blue – and in the bold simplicity of its
composition. Its discovery adds considerable strength to the
theory that Cuyp must have been in early contact with one of
the Haarlem Italianisers. Berchem and Dujardin returned to
Holland in 1645, Hendrik Mommers in 1646; the first of these
is the most likely contact.

46 Muleteers in a hilly landscape
panel 19×29½in./47×73cm., inscribed *A. cuyp*
Cleveland Museum of Art (*Bequest John L. Severance*)
first recorded J. van der Linden van Slingeland sale 1785
painted late 1640s; reference HdG 465
reproduced in colour, plate VI

De Groot's account of this picture is incorrect. He confuses
it with a smaller picture which was in the Lebrun collection,
where it was engraved by Maillet, from thence it came into
the collection of the Earl of Crewe (HdG 470b) and finally to
the Mauritshuis at The Hague. A copy of R46 was in the
Breslau (Wroclaw) museum but is apparently not there now.
A brilliant white strongly contrasted with earth colours is a
characteristic feature of Cuyp's style *circa* 1647.

The influence of Jacob Gerritsz Cuyp

47 Pastoral scene
canvas 44 × 66½in./110 × 166cm., inscribed *J. G. cuyp Fecit*
Montaubon Museum
painted by Jacob Gerritsz Cuyp *circa* 1640

A characteristic example of Jacob Cuyp's early, Bloemaertesque,
landscape style. No later landscapes are acknowledged although
several must exist. This implies his style may have changed
fundamentally during the 1640s and become confused with
that of Aelbert.

48 Orpheus

canvas 59½ × 106½in./149 × 267cm., inscribed *A. cuyp*
The Marquess of Bute
first recorded late eighteenth century
attributed to J. G. Cuyp *circa* 1647; reference HdG 19

By its strong local colouring (the musician is clad in scarlet and mauve) as well as its naïve approach, this picture points unmistakably in the direction of J. G. Cuyp. At the same time, some contribution from Aelbert cannot be ruled out, for instance the crouching mastiff (compare R113). It is also not impossible that Jacob used his son as the model for Orpheus. This would imply either that Aelbert was a musician as well as a painter or that his mastery in representing animals was being symbolized. De Groot has confused the provenance with that of another Orpheus about half the size which passed through the van Nispen and Verschuuring sales in the mid eighteenth century.

The engraving is based on a drawing by Abraham Bloemaert (1564-1651) and was published in 1611. Bloemaert was the teacher of Jacob Gerritsz Cuyp and is clearly seen to be the source of much of the Cuyps' thematic material.

49 Young Sportsman
canvas 38×50in./95×125cm., inscribed *J. G. Cuyp 1646*
Present whereabouts unknown
Last recorded with J. Rochelle Thomas 1928
painted by Jacob Gerritsz Cuyp in 1646

The recumbent greyhound should be compared with that in the
previous picture. According to de Groot, who saw the painting
in 1928, the building in the distance is the St Jacob's Church at
The Hague. The picture is reproduced from an old magazine
advertisement.

50 Four children in a landscape
canvas 41×52in./104×132cm., inscribed *A. cuyp fecit* **1645**
Private collection, Devon
first recorded Bertels sale 1780
attributed to Aelbert Cuyp *circa* 1645

Although this picture shows the influence of J. G. Cuyp,
it is handled in a less direct, extravert manner. Certain
contre-jour elements point towards Aelbert but, as no other
portraits are acknowledged, the attribution can only be tentative.
The inscription may not be in its original condition, but the
facts it states could well be accurate, thus confirming that
Aelbert had come under the influence of the Italianisers at least
by 1645.

51 The Piping Herdsmen
canvas 35½×47in./89×117cm., inscribed *A. cuyp*
Metropolitan Museum, New York
first recorded with Sedelmeyer 1894
Cuyp studio 1640–45; reference HdG 331

If this painting were not completely monochromatic in
colouring, one would have no hesitation in attributing it to
J. G. Cuyp: the two cows just squeezing into the picture and
eyeing the spectator, the small playful dog, the heavy folds of
the draperies: such features are entirely characteristic of the
elder Cuyp. Possibly he reduced his range of colour in
deference to current fashion.

52 Two shepherds with bucking goat
panel 21×27in./53×68cm., inscribed *A. cuyp*
Present whereabouts unknown
first and last recorded Lepke sale 6 December 1934
Cuyp studio 1645–50

The links with J. G. Cuyp are unmistakable but the picture
appears nevertheless to be the work of another hand. As in the
previous picture, Dordrecht is seen from the south-east, the
view being based on a drawing in the Amsterdam
Rijksprentenkabinet (see also R61).

Reproduced from the illustration in the Lepke sale
catalogue.

The engravings are numbers 11 and 12 in J. G. Cuyp's
Diversa Animalia.

53 Shepherds with their flock
panel 19×29in./48×72cm., inscribed *A. cuyp*
Private collection, U.S.A.
first recorded collection Lord Antrobus (present century)
possibly Aelbert Cuyp *circa* 1646

One of a group of paintings related more closely to Aelbert
than to J. G. Cuyp, yet unmistakably deriving from the latter
(compare number 13 in *Diversa Animalia* already reproduced
in association with R15). The two associated figure studies,
on the other hand, are undoubtedly Aelbert's work; the one
shown here was formerly in the Victor de Stuers collection
while the other belongs to F. Lugt (see R64).

54 Landscape with two horses
panel 20 × 26½in./50 × 66cm., inscribed *A. cuyp*
Mittelrheinisches Landesmuseum, Mainz
first recorded van Zaanen sale 1767
Cuyp studio 1645–50; reference HdG 353 and 557

The view over the water-meadows is the same as in the previous
work but seen from a few yards further to the right. This could
imply that two painters were working beside each other. The
panel is thinly painted and was probably once an inch or two
wider. Almost certainly by the same painter as R52.

55 Milking scene

panel 20×26in./50×65cm., inscribed *A. cuyp*
National Gallery of Ireland, Dublin
first recorded J. Gillott sale 1872
Cuyp studio 1645–50; reference HdG 364

Like so many of these pictures it could more easily have been
attributed to Aelbert had it been painted in the late 1630s,
but this is here ruled out by the fact that the preparatory
drawing for the milkmaid belongs unquestionably to the mid
1640s. (It should be noted that this picture is very much
smaller than R56.)

The chalk study was at The Hague.

56 The Milkmaid
canvas 54 × 69in./135 × 172·5cm., inscribed *A. cuyp*
The Duke of Sutherland
first recorded Lord Francis Egerton *circa* 1820
attributed to Aelbert Cuyp *circa* 1646; reference HdG 369

The authority with which this picture is painted suggests it
cannot be the work of a pupil. In many ways it resembles the
large early landscape at Melbury Park (R7) but the rich and
glowing impasto strongly indicates J. G. Cuyp. On the other
hand, the manner of composition does not relate to any known
work by the father. Once again iconological factors clearly
point to the mid 1640s. The correct attribution and dating of
this picture could be fundamental to the unravelment of
Aelbert's early stylistic evolution.

57 Milking scene with haycart
canvas 42×69½in./106×174cm., inscribed *A. cuyp*
Hermitage, Leningrad
first recorded collection Catherine II *circa* 1780
attributed to Aelbert Cuyp *circa* 1647; reference HdG 379

This painting, which is badly worn, compares closely in
colouring and technique with R43. A certain blandness in the
manner of composition suggests the possibility of some contact
with the precocious Paulus Potter (1625–1654) who, by 1646,
was already established in the neighbouring town of Delft.

58 Landscape with haycart

canvas 56 × 89in./140 × 224cm., inscribed *A. cuyp*
John and Mabel Ringling Museum of Art, Sarasota
first recorded van der Potts sale 1825
attributed to Aelbert Cuyp *circa* 1646
reference HdG 216, 359 and 383b

One of the largest canvases by or attributed to Cuyp and in
style much closer to Aelbert than to Jacob, although lacking
the essential chiaroscuro associated with the younger painter's
work from about 1644 onwards. Possibly, therefore, a studio
picture painted under his immediate supervision.

Etching by A. Cuyp reproduced in reverse (D1).

93

59 Piping shepherd, near Leiden
panel 26 × 35in./65 × 88cm.
Present whereabouts unknown
Cuyp studio 1645–50

Two pictures which represent the identical view of Leiden but
which, like R53 and 54, seem clearly to be the work of different
artists. As the Marekerk is not yet visible, they must both have
been painted before 1648. There is a related drawing in the
Amsterdam Rijksprentenkabinet.

60 Shepherd and bucking goat, near Leiden
panel 25½ × 35½in./64 × 89cm., inscribed *A. cuyp*
National Gallery of Victoria, Melbourne
first recorded Lord Huntingfield sale 1916
attributed to A. or J. G. Cuyp *circa* 1646

The curiously mannered handling of the foliage is
characteristic of neither of the Cuyps, yet the picture has
considerable qualities. A general olive-green tonality recalls
the later work of Jacob Gerritsz and, on balance, he seems the
most likely candidate.

61 The kicking horse
panel 26 × 35in./65 × 88cm., inscribed *A. cuyp*
John G. Johnson Collection, Philadelphia
first recorded Amsterdam sale 1811
Cuyp studio 1645–50; reference HdG 361

A clear example of a school picture. The distant landscape is
based on a drawing in the Amsterdam Rijksprentenkabinet
(see also R51 and 52).

62 Sheep and cattle near Dordrecht
panel 19 × 28½in./47 × 71cm., inscribed *A. cuyp*
Willem van der Vorm Foundation, Museum Boymans-van
Beuningen, Rotterdam
first recorded Cook collection *circa* 1900
Cuyp studio 1645–50; reference HdG 707

Dordrecht is here seen from the south-west, in other words
from the direction of Dubbledam, where Cuyp later possessed
a country house. The view is based on a drawing in the British
Museum, which also did service for two paintings in Cuyp's
mature style (R79 and 83). This tends to suggest that this picture,
although 'early' in character, may not have been painted
before 1650.

The drawing seems also to have been the basis of an
engraving by Rademaker (*Kabinet van Nederlandsche Outheden
en Gezichten*, 1725, II 134) which purports to represent
Dordrecht in the year 1650.

97

63 Pasture beside a river
panel $28\frac{1}{2} \times 42\frac{1}{2}$in./$71 \times 106$cm., inscribed *A. cuyp*
Lord Egremont, Petworth
first recorded at Petworth 1848
Cuyp studio 1645–50; reference HdG 706

The cow being milked should be compared with R43 which
again suggests a date towards the end of the 1640s. The
colouring is rich and warm but, as de Groot says, the trees
are somewhat unskilfully drawn. The inscription appears on a
plank (see also R28, 32, 33 and 34).

64 Pasture near Utrecht

panel 20×30in./50×75cm., inscribed *A. cuyp*
Amsterdam sale, *1971*
first recorded Lord Berwick sale 1825
Cuyp studio 1645–50; reference HdG 259 and 709

Even allowing for the poor condition, this picture seems to
have been painted rather timidly. The colouring is warm in
tone. The buildings have been recognised as the Duitse Kapel
and the Mariabolwerk at Utrecht; there is a related drawing in
Berlin.

The back-turned figure is based on a drawing in the Lugt
collection; the other figure in this drawing appears in R53.

65 Interior of a cowshed

panel 30×41in./75×102cm., inscribed *A. cuyp*
National Museum, Stockholm
first recorded Lord Gwydyr sale 1829
Cuyp studio 1645–50; reference HdG 754

Of the many stable scenes and cowsheds which have been
ascribed to Cuyp these two appear to be strongest candidates;
yet they are very different in style. On balance, R66 is the more
convincing.

66 Cowshed with open door
panel $20\frac{1}{2} \times 26\frac{1}{2}$in./51 $\times$ 67cm., inscribed *A. cuyp*
Private collection, France
first recorded Usselino sale 1866
attributed to Aelbert Cuyp *circa* 1644
reference HdG 758 and 763a

The style of the distant landscape suggests that this picture
belongs to Cuyp's van Goyenesque period.

67 Cows and sheep near a river
canvas 41 × 58in./102 × 145cm.
Present whereabouts unknown
first recorded Lord Clinton sale 1950
Cuyp follower 1645-50

A fairly large, incompetently painted, canvas which appears
to lie on the fringe of the Cuyp school.

68 The Musical herdsmen
canvas 40×52in./100×130cm., inscribed *A. cuyp 1646*
Leon Sergold, New York
first recorded collection Count Suboff *circa* 1925
Cuyp follower 1645-50

Apparently the work of a Utrecht follower of Cuyp. The
inscription is quite clearly false; nevertheless the picture might
well have been painted in the year stated: 1646.

69 Woodland scene, artist sketching
canvas $38\frac{1}{2}\times53\frac{1}{2}$in./96×134cm., inscribed *A. cuyp*
London sale, 27 March 1968
first recorded collection Mrs M. G. Young *circa* 1640
Cuyp studio 1645–50

Another picture on the fringe of the early Cuyp school (*see*
R67 and 68), and possibly a collaboration between two artists.
The figures call to mind the work of Jan Olis (*circa* 1610–76)
and J. F. van der Merck (*circa* 1610–64).

70 Merwede tower, artist sketching
panel 19½ × 26½in./49 × 66cm.
Art Gallery, Strasbourg
first recorded General Craig sale 1812
Cuyp studio *circa* 1650; reference HdG 74 and 78

The work of an able imitator of Aelbert Cuyp but too thinly
painted to be authentic. Compare R40.

Cattle pieces

71 Herdsman driving cattle
panel 28 × 36in./70·5 × 91cm., inscribed *A. cuyp*
National Trust, Waddesdon Manor
first recorded collection Ralph Willett (died 1795)
painted late 1640s; reference HdG 417 and 419

In about 1648, Cuyp came to realise that the most powerful
effects of light could be obtained when the sky is heavily
overcast (there was an exactly parallel development in the art
of Paulus Potter). In this case the exaggerated sunset effect
shows it to be one of the earliest examples of its kind. The town
in the distance is The Hague where, as it happens, Potter was
also working at about this date.

72 Cattle, the passing storm
panel 32×26in./80×62cm., inscribed *A. cuyp*
Mrs M. M. Fry, Saffron Walden
first recorded collection William Wells 1834
painted late 1640s; reference HdG 186 and 270

Cuyp made much use of earth colours at this stage of his
career: browns, greys, heavy greens and ochres.
Gainsborough's free transcription of the picture
(*see* p. 11) shows that it must already have been in England
well before the end of the eighteenth century.

73 Five cows with herdsman
canvas 36×44in./90×135cm., inscribed *A. cuyp*
The Earl of Harrowby
first recorded Prestage sale 1761
painted late 1640s; reference HdG 264

The grouping of the cattle is unfamiliar but in other respects
the picture is characteristic of the period. It is considerably
larger than the painting opposite.

  Etching by A. Cuyp reproduced in reverse (D5).

74 Four cows below an escarpment
octagonal panel 8 × 9½in./20 × 24cm., inscribed *A. cuyp*
B. de Geus van den Heuvel, Amsterdam
first recorded (possibly) Jacob Houcke sale 1669
painted late 1640s; reference HdG 198

If this tiny panel was really in the sale of the surgeon
Jacob Houcke in 1669, it has a longer recorded history than
any of Cuyp's paintings. It was engraved by Pye in 1774.
The sky is lighter than in most of the paintings of the period.

75 Cattle beside a river, moonlight
Present whereabouts unknown
engraved in mezzotint by William Baillie 1773
reference HdG 730

Houbraken's account of the artist (*see* p. 198) suggests that
he painted several moonlight scenes. Iconographically this
appears to be a promising candidate.

76 Seven cows on a river bank
panel 28 × 36in./71 × 90·5cm., inscribed *A. cuyp*
Residenz-Galerie, Salzburg
first recorded Czernin collection 1834
painted late 1640s; reference HdG 227

The same grouping of the cattle appears in R72 and R75,
also in a large number of replicas with slight variations.

77 Moonlit river scene, with cattle
panel 19×28in./48×70cm.
Possibly still with the Grosvenor family
first recorded Dr. Bragge sale 1759
reference HdG 724

Another moonlight scene which looks convincing from this
early line engraving (*see* note to R75). It was bought by Sir
Richard Grosvenor at the Bragge sale in 1759.

78 Five cows below a steep bank
panel 16 × 24in./40 × 60cm., inscribed *A. cuyp*
Present whereabouts unknown
first recorded collection William Wells 1834
painted late 1640s; reference HdG 394

Cuyp's cattle pieces have always been more popular with
painters than collectors. They were so extensively imitated in
the nineteenth century that it is now difficult to realise how
original they were at the time they were painted.

79 Cattle near Dordrecht (The Small Dort)
panel 26×39in./66×100cm., inscribed *A. cuyp*
National Gallery, London (by courtesy of the Trustees)
first recorded (possibly) Captain Baillie sale 1771
painted late 1640s; reference HdG 342

One of the less interesting paintings of this period in Cuyp's
development. See note to R83.

80 Milking scene, stormy sky
panel 30 × 42in./75 × 105cm., inscribed *A. cuyp*
Dulwich College Picture Gallery, London
Desenfans bequest 1811
painted late 1640s; reference HdG 201a

A much finer painting than appears from the reproduction,
with a strong sense of light. There are other versions in the
Boymans-van Beuningen Museum at Rotterdam (HdG 384)
and in the museum at San Diego (HdG 385)

The related drawing was sold at Sotheby's on 21 October
1963.

81 Two anglers and cattle on a river bank
panel 20×32in./50×80cm., inscribed *A. cuyp*
Probably with the de Rothschild family, Paris
first recorded Marquess of Camden sale 1841
reference HdG 323 and 327

This line engraving, made at the time of the San Donato sale
in 1868, represents what is probably the original version of
a much copied composition. The nearest cow also appears in
R43 and R44.

82 Cows with seated herdsman
panel 19½×29in./49×73cm., inscribed *A. cuyp*
Frick Collection, New York
first recorded (possibly) N. Nieuhoff sale 1777
reference HdG 212, 230 and 302

This picture has a thick, insensitive paint texture which
suggests either that it is a copy or that it has been heavily
restored. As the Nieuhoff sale catalogue mentions a copse and
several vessels on the river, it may well have been describing
a slightly different picture.

83 Cattle near Dordrecht (The Large Dort)
canvas $62 \times 77\frac{1}{2}$in./157×197cm., inscribed *A. cuyp*
National Gallery, London (by courtesy of the Trustees)
first recorded collection Sir Henry Bruce 1849
painted late 1640s; reference HdG 268e and 368

In this picture, Cuyp reached his furthest point in the
representation of sheer bulk. There is a related drawing in
the British Museum (*see* also R62 and R79).
 Etching by A. Cuyp reproduced in reverse (D2).

84 The Piping Herdsmen
canvas 68×91½in./171×229cm., inscribed *A. cuyp*
The Louvre, Paris
first recorded collection Louis XVI in 1783
painted late 1640s; reference HdG 332

A work of comparable solidity to R83 and one of the largest
pictures Cuyp painted. In the distance can be seen the tower
of the church at Rhenen.
   Etching by A. Cuyp reproduced in reverse (D7).

85 Cattle watering, left bank
panel 23½ × 29½in./59 × 74cm., inscribed *A. cuyp*
Museum of Fine Arts, Budapest
first recorded Hankey sale 1799
painted *circa* 1650; reference HdG 390

This and especially R86 are among Cuyp's finest paintings.
They achieve a kind of perfection which must have inhibited
further exploration of this particular theme.
    Etching by A. Cuyp reproduced in reverse (D3).

86 Cattle watering, right bank
panel $23\frac{1}{2} \times 29$in./$59 \times 72\cdot5$cm., inscribed *A. cuyp*
D. J. Robarts, London
first recorded Lord Radstock sale 1826
painted *circa* 1650; reference HdG 393

This subject appears in many versions; generally they follow
R87 rather than this picture, possibly because the latter was
engraved in 1767. No painting embodies more completely
the qualities for which Cuyp is most valued.

87 Cattle watering, right bank (small version)
panel 15×22in./37·5×55cm.
Hermitage, Leningrad
engraved by H. J. Antonissen in 1767
reference HdG 396

The exact relationship between this picture and R86 is difficult
to determine. If the present work is genuine, it seems clear
it must be the earlier, being weaker both in design and
chiaroscuro.

Antonissen's engraving is reproduced in reverse.

88 River scene with cattle and anglers
panel 18 × 29½in./45 × 74cm., inscribed *A. cuyp*
National Gallery, London (by courtesy of the Trustees)
first recorded Nogaret sale 1780
painted *circa* 1650; reference HdG 325, 328 and 391
reproduced in colour, plate VII

A picture of comparable quality to R86 and very close in
style to the two other classic paintings of this period: the *View
of Dordrecht* (R98) and *The river crossing* (R96).

89 Landscape with cattle, horsemen and peasants
panel 19×32½in./48×72cm., inscribed *A. cuyp*
Corcoran Gallery of Art, Washington (W. A. Clark Collection)
first recorded collection Earl of Carlisle 1815
reference HdG 424

A somewhat eclectic composition which represents a kind of
compromise between the straightforward cattle-piece and the
style of Cuyp's later equestrian landscapes. There are points of
comparison with HdG 427 (National Gallery, London), a
picture which has certain anachronistic features.

90 Cattle with horseman and peasants
panel 15 × 20in./38 × 50cm., inscribed *A. cuyp*
National Gallery, London (by courtesy of the Trustees)
first recorded collection William Herring 1754
painted early 1650s; reference HdG 429 and 446

A painting in a much lighter key than the previous cattle
pieces and possessing certain decorative features which suggest
the somewhat later date. It was engraved by Vivares in 1754.
In the distance can be seen the Merwede tower. No picture
gives a clearer idea of Cuyp's ability to simplify the most
complex forms and reinterpret them in terms of light. Note the
shadow cast by the cow's horns, an illusionist device of which
the painter was particularly fond.

91 Milking scene with approaching horseman
canvas $46\frac{1}{2} \times 64\frac{1}{2}$in./117 × 162cm., inscribed *A. cuyp*
Washington University Gallery of Art, St. Louis
first recorded London sale 1907
painted mid 1650s; reference HdG 378 (part incorrect)

Although conceived on a comparable scale to R83 and 84,
this painting again possesses certain decorative characteristics
which point to a somewhat later date. The town in the distance
is The Hague. The version of this picture described by Smith
(231) was still at Alscot (not Alcote) in 1965.
    Etching by A. Cuyp reproduced in reverse (D6).

92 Pointing herdsman, seven cows
canvas $26 \times 34\frac{1}{2}$in./66×88cm., inscribed *A. cuyp*
National Gallery, Washington (Andrew Mellon Collection)
first recorded collection Henry Penton 1760
painted mid 1650s; reference HdG 203

Another cattle piece painted at a time when Cuyp had become
concerned with elegance of design rather than the realistic
interpretation of the subject. It was engraved by Vivares in
1760.

River scenes and ice scenes

93 Shipping on the Maas
canvas $39 \times 53\frac{1}{2}$in./98×135cm.
Wallace Collection, London
first recorded Delahante sale 1811
painted late 1640s; reference HdG 34 and 167b

Diffuse both in composition and colour, it may, as de Groot
suggested, be considerably worn in parts. It belongs to the
period, *circa* 1647, when the painter was experimenting with
effects of sunset and sunrise, in this case the latter. Compare
R44.

94 Dordrecht, sunrise
canvas 42 × 65in./105 × 162·5cm., inscribed *A. cuyp*
Frick Collection, New York
first recorded (possibly) Bertels sale 1775 (No. 53)
painted late 1640s
Reproduced in colour, plate V

A more successful painting of the same date as R93, it again
represents dawn. It belongs strictly to Cuyp's *contre-jour*
period but has been placed with the main group of marine
subjects for convenience of reference. The view of the town
is identical with that appearing in the severed picture, R29/30.

95 Shipping on the Maas, officer embarking
canvas $43 \times 59\frac{1}{2}$in./107×148cm., inscribed *A. cuyp*
David Robarts, London
first recorded Robarts collection 1834
painted *circa* 1650; reference HdG 32 and 33

A work comparable to R93 but, in every respect,
more vigorous.

96 The river crossing

panel $27\frac{1}{2} \times 35$in./69×87cm., inscribed *A. cuyp*
Wallace Collection, London
first recorded collection Sir Robert Price 1837
painted early 1650s; reference HdG 640

One of the classic paintings of Cuyp's early maturity, others being the two cattle pieces R86 and 88, and the Ascott *View of Dordrecht* (R98). The composition, seemingly so natural, is one of remarkable originality. Both Smith and de Groot were mistaken in supposing this picture to have been part of the Slingeland collection, confusing it with HdG 633 (R100). The related drawing is in Berlin.

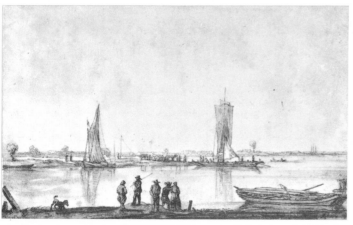

97 Dordrecht, evening
canvas 39×55in./98×138cm., inscribed *A. cuyp*
Kenwood House, London
first recorded collection Nieuwenhuys 1829
painted early 1650s; reference HdG 165 and 631

One of the many Cuyp mysteries is the exact relationship
between these two pictures. Although an exceptionally fine
painting, R97 seems almost crude by comparison with the
Ascott picture. We need only draw attention to two details:
firstly the tilt of the two-masted schooner, and secondly the
light on the houses on the extreme right of the town. There is,
of course, no question of one being copied from the other. It is
almost as though two artists had painted the same scene
simultaneously but from slightly different angles. As the angle

chosen for the shipping piece at Washington (R104) follows
the Kenwood picture, it can be argued that R97 must be the
later of the two versions.

98 View of Dordrecht
canvas 27 × 76in./68·5 × 190cm.
National Trust, Ascott
first recorded Sir George Colebrooke sale 1774
painted early 1650s; reference HdG 164

This picture, one of Cuyp's supreme masterpieces, had already
been cut in half by the time it appeared in the Colebrooke
sale of 1774. The question to be considered is whether, like the
earlier view of Dordrecht (R29/30), it lost some of its sky in the
process. Although it was clearly intended to have a panoramic
character, we cannot help feeling that the bowl of light at the
apex of the sky was not meant to be severed quite so abruptly.
Both R97 and 98 represent Dordrecht in the late afternoon
and are exceptional in that the sun is on the right of the picture.

99 The Passage Boat
canvas 49 × 57in./122 × 142cm., inscribed *A. cuyp*
Royal Collection, Buckingham Palace
first recorded collection George IV in 1814
painted early 1650s; reference HdG 637

Cuyp often distorted proportions to give emphasis to the particular character of the subject he was presenting; in this case, the diminutive figures on the jetty and the dwarf who holds the sail add greatly to the effectiveness of the picture as a whole. This picture is considerably larger than the panel on the facing page.

100 The Rotterdam Ferry
panel 24 × 30in./60 × 75cm., inscribed *A. cuyp*
Frick Collection, New York
first recorded collection J. van der Linden van Slingeland 1752
painted early 1650s; reference HdG 633 and 640.

According to Hoet's description (*Catalogus of Naamlyst var Schildereyen 1752* II p. 490), this picture represents the Rotterdam ferry passing Alblasserdam, a village a few miles north of Dordrecht. Hofstede de Groot confused the provenance of this picture with that of R96.

101 Maas at Dordrecht, thunderstorm
panel 20×29in./49×73cm., inscribed *A. cuyp*
National Gallery, London (by courtesy of the Trustees)
first recorded collection Prince Regent *circa* 1810
painted early 1650s; reference HdG 167c and 636

This has generally been considered an early work but it is
difficult not to associate it with the next picture which clearly
belongs to Cuyp's maturity. The style is unfamiliar simply
because the painter made so few sketches in his later period.

102 The Maas, a stiff breeze

canvas 38 × 58½in./95 × 148cm., inscribed *A. cuyp*
Wallace Collection, London
first recorded collection J. van der Linden van Slingeland 1752
painted early 1650s; reference HdG 639

Cuyp very rarely painted rough water and this, together witn
its sketch, may well be the sole examples from this stage of his
career. There are, however, a number of other versions of the
same subject, all apparently the work of imitators. The picture
is heavily concealed by discoloured varnish.

103 Prince Frederick Henry at Nijmegen

canvas $45\frac{1}{2} \times 66\frac{1}{2}$in./$114 \times 166$cm.
The Duke of Sutherland
first recorded (possibly) Colebrooke sale 1774
painted mid 1650s; reference HdG 30 and 175a

Both in this picture and in R107, the distinguished person in
the ten-oared boat can be identified as Prince Frederick Henry
(see notes to R147 and 148). Although the Prince died in 1647,
several years before these pictures were painted, his triumphal
visits to Dordrecht must have made a deep impression on Cuyp
as a young man, and it is not surprising he should have wished
to record such events at a later date. Smith and de Groot were
however mistaken in supposing these two pictures, R103 and
R106, were once pendants in the famous Slingeland collection.
The two paintings in question were R104 and R106, while
R103 was probably the picture which sold for two hundred
and ninety guineas (an easy Cuyp record at the time) in the
Cclebrooke sale of 1774. Although simply described in the
catalogue as a view of Nijmegen, it was again referred to in a
catalogue of 27 April 1780 in connection with another shipping
piece: 'A view on the water near Dort, representing a calm
with a multitude of vessels and boats floating . . . and may be
deemed equal to the picture of his (a view near Nimweggen)
which sold in Sir George Colebrook's sale for three hundred
guineas'.

104 The Maas at Dordrecht
canvas 46 × 66½in./115 × 166cm., inscribed *A. cuyp*
National Gallery of Art, Washington (Andrew Mellon Collection)
first recorded collection J. van der Linden van Slingeland 1752
painted mid 1650s; reference HdG 28
reproduced in colour, plate VIII

Smith considered this to be Cuyp's finest painting. If put to
the test, this verdict might well be confirmed today, although
R98, 103, 139 and 140 would certainly be close competitors.
The fact that this picture and R106 hung as pendants in the
Slingeland collection is by no means proof that they were
painted as such. In both cases, the distinguished visitor
appears to be departing and there is no clear evidence that
Frederick Henry is the subject of R104. It is interesting to note
that the large passage boat exactly repeats the format of the
anchored sailing vessel in the early river scene, R32.

105 A landing party
panel 28 × 35½in./70·5 × 89cm., inscribed *A. cuyp*
National Trust, Waddesdon Manor
first recorded J. Goll van Franckenstein sale 1833
painted mid 1650s; reference HdG 31 and 647

Despite their superlative qualities, these two pictures are not
modelled with quite the same strength as their predecessors
(R103 and 104); the colour is attractive but lacks plasticity
and has the effect almost of weakening the overall sense of
light. This implies that they were painted at a somewhat later
date, when Cuyp's approach was tending increasingly towards
the decorative.

106 Prince Frederick Henry at Dordrecht
canvas $45\frac{1}{2} \times 66\frac{1}{2}$in./$114 \times 166$cm.
National Trust, Waddesdon Manor
first recorded collection J. van der Linden van Slingeland 1752
painted mid 1650s; reference HdG 36

This picture probably represents Prince Frederick Henry,
Stadholder and Admiral General of the United Provinces,
inspecting the Dutch fleet before it set out for Flanders via
Zeeland in June 1646. Simon de Vlieger also painted this
subject three times (Vienna, Budapest and Cambridge). One
suspects that, if Cuyp had any political sympathies, they
would certainly have been royalist. This is implied by the fact
that his name was among those from which William III chose
the regency of Dordrecht in 1672; his orthodox Calvinism
and friendship with Cornelis van Beveren also point in this
direction.

107 View on the Rhine
panel 11 × 15in./27·5 × 36·5cm., inscribed *A. cuyp*
Institut Néerlandais, Paris (*F. Lugt collection*)
first recorded collection Sir Luke Schaub 1751
painted mid 1650s; reference HdG 658

This picture appears in three versions, all of which have been
confidently accepted as authentic: the two paintings here
reproduced, and another belonging to the Staatliches Museum,
Berlin-Dahlem (HdG 388) which exactly follows the Rotterdam
picture except that it is slightly smaller (12 × 15½in.). The
present work appears to be a sketch, and is paler and more
atmospheric in colouring than any other painting of Cuyp's
maturity.

108 View on the Rhine
panel $16 \times 21\frac{1}{2}$in./40×54cm., remains of inscription
Museum Boymans-van Beuningen, Rotterdam
first recorded collection Boymans 1811
painted mid 1650s; reference HdG 397, see also HdG 725c

It is just possible that, when covered by dark varnish, this
picture might once have been mistaken for a moonlight; in
which case it could be linked with the painting in the Slingeland
collection (HdG 725c). Its sharp, strong colouring suggests a
late date.

109 The Waal at Nijmegen
panel 18 × 22in./44·6 × 55·4cm., inscribed *A. cuyp*
De Rothschild, Paris, in 1939
first recorded collection Jeremiah Harman 1834
painted mid 1650s; reference HdG 659e

One of the most highly prized pictures of the early nineteenth
century, it connects closely with the large shipping piece in the
Sutherland collection (R103). It could be a preliminary study
for this painting or it may be a later derivation. According to
the conception of the painter's stylistic development here
proposed, that he progressed towards a greater simplicity of
construction, the latter hypothesis seems the more likely. The
view of the town and the Valkhof contain several elements of
fantasy.

110 Dordrecht at dawn
panel 18×26in./45×65cm.
Private collection, London
first recorded collection Duke of Westminster 1821
painted mid 1650s; reference HdG 641
reproduced in colour, plate IX

As John Smith wrote in 1834: 'This simple scene, by the magical diffusion of light and heat, together with a skilful arrangement of colour, possesses a charm which rivets the attention and admiration of every beholder'. He was, however, incorrect in believing it to represent evening. The tower is, of course, the Groothofdspoort. The classic simplicity of the composition fulfils the apparent aspirations of R105 and 106.

There is a similar composition, which also owes something to R105 and 106, in the Toronto Gallery (HdG 652 and 665); possibly it is the work of a follower working under Cuyp's direct supervision.

111 The frozen Maas, Merwede tower
panel 25½×35½in./64×89cm., inscribed *A. cuyp*
The Earl of Yarborough
first recorded collection J. van der Linden van Slingeland 1752
painted early 1650s; reference HdG 737

It is suggested that this is the earlier of Cuyp's two most
famous ice scenes on the grounds that the handling is broader
than that of the Bedford picture. Another version (HdG 740),
with several variations, was sold in London on 5 November
1966 (ex collection Earl Howe).

112 The Maas in winter
panel 23×46in./57×115cm., inscribed *A. cuyp*
The Duke of Bedford
first recorded Bryan sale 1804
painted late 1650s; reference HdG 733 and 739b

No paintings by Cuyp are more resplendent with a sense of
light than these two winter scenes. A good copy of this picture
is in the San Francisco Museum (HdG 740a).

Equestrian subjects

113 The Negro Page
canvas 56 × 89in./140 × 222·5cm.
Royal Collection, Buckingham Palace
first recorded J. Bertels sale 1788
painted late 1640s; reference HdG 549

The early date of this picture is established not merely by the
costume but also by comparison with the painting of the dogs
which appear in R48 and 49. Like the *Large Dort* in the
National Gallery (R83), it marks the culmination of the
painter's attempt to achieve sheer solidity of construction.
The horse brass in the form of a *fleur-de-lys* suggests that the
gentleman with the black hat is one of the sons of Cornelis
van Beveren, possibly Willem his eldest son, who was born in
1624.

114 The Trooper
canvas 46 × 58½ in./115 × 146cm., inscribed *A. cuyp*
Royal Collection, Buckingham Palace
first recorded collection Prince Regent *circa* 1805
painted early 1650s; reference HdG 550

It is significant, again from the point of view of dating, that,
with the exception of the *Baptism of the Eunuch* (R118),
all equestrian paintings subsequent to *The Negro Page* (R113)
show the light falling at right-angles to the line of vision.

115 Halt at an inn near Rhenen
canvas 24 × 33½in./60 × 84cm., inscribed *A. cuyp*
Present whereabouts unknown
first recorded Hobbs sale 1764
painted early 1650s; reference HdG 517

There appears to be no surviving drawing for this attractive
view of Rhenen; nor, apparently, was it ever used again by
the painter. The picture was acquired by the Duke of
Marlborough in 1764. It was with the dealer Bachstitz in 1949.

116 Two horsemen, one dismounted
panel $14\frac{1}{2} \times 18\frac{1}{2}$in./$36 \times 46$cm., inscribed *A. cuyp*
Royal Collection, Buckingham Palace
first recorded collection Baring 1814
painted early 1650s; reference HdG 488

Two characteristic cabinet pictures of the kind which was later much imitated by the Calraets and other painters of the Cuyp school.

117 Halt at an inn, wooded country
panel 18×28in./45×70cm., inscribed *A. cuyp*
M. Knoedler & Co. 1926
first recorded collection Tolozan 1801
painted early 1650s; reference HdG 511 and 527

The drawing for this picture is in the Albertina, Vienna. Such paintings are difficult to date with accuracy and might well have been produced at any time during the 1650s.

118 The Baptism of the Eunuch
canvas 44×65in./109×162cm., inscribed *A. cuyp*
National Trust, Anglesey Abbey
first recorded Comte de Vismes sale 1786
painted early 1650s; reference HdG 11 and 12

The heaviness of the foliage and the diagonal fall of light
suggest that this picture cannot have been painted much later
than *The Negro Page* (R113).

119 The Avenue at Meerdervoort
canvas $27\frac{1}{2} \times 38\frac{1}{2}$in./$70 \times 98$cm., inscribed *A. cuyp*
Wallace Collection, London
first recorded Smeth van Alphen sale 1816
painted early 1650s; reference HdG 168

It has been suggested (*see* p. 9) that the two boys in the
distance must be Michiel and Cornelis Pompe van Meerdervoort
and that the picture was therefore painted in about 1652.
Although far from one of the finest of Cuyp's paintings, it
established in 1868 the record price for a landscape by an
artist of any school.

120 Cavaliers halted, one sketching
panel 19 × 32in./47·5 × 80cm., inscribed *A. cuyp*
The Duke of Bedford
first recorded John Bertels sale 1775
painted early 1650s; reference HdG 72

An unusually direct transcript from nature representing the
countryside near Elten on the borders of Holland and Germany.
There are several associated drawings and other versions of the
picture, some showing the two figures on the left of the
landscape. This, however, is the finest example and the only
one whose authenticity can be accepted with certainty.

121 Two young horsemen with their tutor
canvas $43 \times 61\frac{1}{2}$in./108×154cm., inscribed *A. cuyp fecit*
Metropolitan Museum, New York
first recorded Chateau de Meerdervoort 1680
painted 1652–3; reference HdG 85 and 617

This picture represents two boys of the Pompe van
Meerdervoort family, Michiel (1638–53) and Cornelis (1639–80),
with their tutor Caulier. It was in the inventory taken on the
death of Cornelis that the picture was recorded (see A. Staring
*Mededelingen van het Rijksbureau voor Kunsthistorische
Documentatie* 1953 p. 117). The landscape in the background
is the same as that seen in R120.

122 Huntsmen halted
canvas $36\frac{1}{2} \times 51\frac{1}{2}$in./$92 \times 129$cm.
Barber Institute of Fine Arts, Birmingham
first recorded London sale 1813
painted early 1650s; reference HdG 627

The huntsmen can be identified by means of the *fleur-de-lys*
emblazoned on the saddle-cloth of the nearest horse as the
three sons of Cornelis van Beveren: Willem (b. 1624), Jan
(b. 1626), and Cornelis (b. *circa* 1630). It is believed that van
Beveren was Cuyp's principal patron (*see* p. 9). The
small-headed horses were a special breed now extinct.

123 The three huntsmen
canvas 41×57in./102·5×142·5cm., inscribed *A. cuyp*
Charles C. Hickox, New York
first recorded collection Duke of Leinster 1909
painted early 1650s; reference HdG 484

It is believed that this picture and R122 inspired a number of
equestrian pieces and portraits of horses, few of which have
quite sufficient brilliance or linear panache to put them beyond
the category of school pictures, for instance HdG 490, 491,
509, 561 (perhaps the finest of the group) and 679.
J. Nieuwstraten has shown an intriguing relationship between
R123, HdG 491 and a drawing in the British Museum by
Claude Lorrain (*Oud Holland* 1965 page 192).

Detail of **The Negro Page** (R113)

Detail of **Lady and gentleman on horseback** (R124)

124 Lady and gentleman on horseback
canvas 47 × 66½in./108 × 166cm., inscribed *A. Cuyp*
National Gallery of Art, Washington (Widener Collection)
first recorded T. Emmerson sale 1832
painted early 1660s; reference HdG 618
reproduced in colour, plate XII

When Hofstede de Groot produced his Catalogue Raisonné the artificiality of Cuyp's later manner was unfashionable but to contemporary taste it makes a strong appeal. Solidity, relief and the illusion of reality, as such, no longer concern the painter; he seems now only interested in the abstract values of painting, the articulation of line and simplicity of contour. The fundamental nature of the change which has taken place during the ten years, 1650–60, is illustrated by the details opposite.

The brass star on the gentleman's horse suggests that he may be a member of the Pompe family, perhaps Cornelis Pompe, the younger of the two boys seen in the New York picture (R121). X-ray photographs show that there has been some overpainting of the two heads. It is interesting to note that this is the only picture listed with the Cuyp signature spelt with a large C.

Other landscapes

125 Soldiers playing cards
panel $18\frac{1}{2}\times28\frac{1}{2}$in./$46\times71$cm., inscribed *A. cuyp*
Art trade, New York 1936
first recorded Beckford, Fonthill Abbey, sale 1823
painted early 1650s; reference HdG 59b

Although this and the next painting contain strong *contre-jour*
elements, they are more stylized than, for instance, *The Negro
Page* (R113), and may be later than their subject-matter would
suggest. The landscape can be recognized as the
neighbourhood of Elten (see R120 and R121).

126 Shepherd and his flock
panel 19½×29½in./48×73cm., inscribed *A. cuyp*
Städelsches Kunstinstitut, Frankfurt
first recorded Delahante sale 1821
painted early 1650s; reference HdG 193

The foreground figure goes right back to Cuyp's earliest
period (R1, 14, etc.). These two paintings (R125 and 126)
may be compared with the Yarborough ice-scene (R111).
The artist's obvious concern with the structure of the
composition make it difficult to give the picture a date earlier
than 1650.

127 View of Nijmegen
canvas $42\frac{1}{2} \times 66$in./106×165cm., inscribed *A. cuyp*
The Duke of Bedford
first recorded Rigby sale 1789
painted mid 1650s; reference HdG 175 and 175b

Many of Cuyp's later landscapes and river-scenes were painted
on canvases approximately 44 by 66in. (110×165cm.). Some
may have been intended as pendants, or it may simply have
been that this was the size which best suited his purpose. As
most of his panels are approximately 19 by 29, it is clear that
he particularly favoured the 2/3 proportion. This leads us to
suggest that this picture may have lost two inches of sky.

128 The Valkhof, Nijmegen
canvas 45 × 66in./113 × 165cm., inscribed *A. cuyp*
National Gallery of Scotland, Edinburgh
first recorded collection Earl of Ashburnham 1834
painted mid 1650s; reference HdG 173 and 174

De Groot was under the mistaken impression that there were
two identical versions of this picture, differing only in size. The
picture in fact changed hands at the time he was preparing his
catalogue, Lady Ashburnham selling to A. de Rothschild.
(The painting in the Newington Hughes sale of 1848 was not
HdG 173 but HdG 420.) There is a preparatory drawing in the
J. P. Morgan collection. Both picture and drawing show only
the southwest corner of the Valkhof complex.

129 The Valkhof, Nijmegen, from the east
panel $19 \times 29\frac{1}{2}$in./48×74cm., inscribed *A. cuyp*
Probably de Rothschild, Paris
Apparently unrecorded until present century

This picture, which was recovered from the Adolf Hitler collection, is known only from a poor photograph. Nevertheless, it has all the characteristics of a genuine work by Cuyp, and is evidently based on the drawing in the British Museum (Hind 19).

130 View of Nijmegen (small version)
panel 18½ × 28in./47 × 70cm., inscribed *A. cuyp*
Indianapolis Museum of Art (Gift in commemoration of the
Sixtieth Anniversary of the Art Association of Indianapolis in
memory of Daniel W. and Elizabeth C. Marmon).
first recorded Gotha Museum 1863
painted mid 1650s; reference HdG 196

This completes the group of Nijmegen paintings, all of which
are based on drawings apparently made in about 1650. A fuller
interpretation must await the forthcoming book on Cuyp's
drawings by J. G. van Gelder and Ingrid Jost.

131 Hilly landscape with horseman
panel 17 × 20in./42·5 × 51cm.
National Museum of Wales, Cardiff
first recorded collection Earl of Carlisle 1815
painted mid 1650s; reference HdG 423

This and R132 are perfect examples of cabinet pictures in
Cuyp's mature Italianate style. There exists a copy of the
painting by Smith of Chichester (1714–76) which shows that it
was already in this country well before the date recorded. The
ruin in the distance is said to be Ubbergen Castle. There are
many versions of the subject, some in reverse, but this is the
only one which appears totally convincing.

132 Ubbergen Castle
panel 12½×21½in./32×54cm.
National Gallery, London
first recorded de Preuil sale 1811
painted mid 1650s; reference HdG 176

The painting is based on a drawing (Albertina, Vienna) which
Cuyp has closely followed. The style is already distinctly 'late'.

133 River landscape, horsemen and peasants
canvas 40×60½in./100×151cm., inscribed *A. cuyp*
Royal Collection, Buckingham Palace
first recorded J. van der Linden van Slingeland sale 1785
painted late 1650s; reference HdG 432

It is interesting to note that, in the next six paintings, Cuyp reverts to a diagonal thrust of light. This factor, together with the very tall trees, suggests a renewed contact with the work of Jan Both. It could be significant that Berchem also painted a number of pastiches of Both at about this time. Another painter who is relevant in this context is Adam Pynacker (1622–73), whose 'Italian landscape with bridge' (Dulwich College Picture Gallery, London) is here reproduced.

134 Three horsemen, herdsmen and shepherdess
canvas 40 × 64in./100 × 164cm., inscribed *A. cuyp*
London sale, 29 June 1973
first recorded van der Gucht sale 1796
painted late 1650s; reference HdG 236a and 415

A painting much in the style of R133 and R138, and admirably
described by Wolfgang Stechow in his *Dutch Landscape
Painting* 1966, page 162: 'One of the glories of this picture –
as of some others of this kind – is the gradual warming up of
its tone from the cool, though sunny, pearl-grey background
(with a 'Mediterranean' city) to the warmer olive-golden tints
in the right foreground; a wonderful clarity permeates every
corner of the picture, with a dominating light blue in the sky,
crisp foliage in silhouette, and red, blue and gold-brown
nuances holding their own in the figures'. The many false
pictures attributed to Cuyp have obscured the fact that he is a
truly magnificent colourist. The price realised by this picture
in June 1973 – £609,000 – has practically restored Cuyp to
his old pre-eminence in the market. It is interesting to note
that it is almost exactly a thousand times the £624 it fetched
in 1796, also in its day a record auction price for the painter.
Among numerous copies is one in the museum at Raleigh.

135 The riding lesson
canvas $46\frac{1}{2} \times 67$in./117×167cm., inscribed *A. cuyp*
Museum of Art, Toledo (Gift of Edward Drummond Libbey)
first recorded collection J. van der Linden van Slingeland 1752
painted late 1650s; reference HdG 448 and 615

A painting over which it is difficult to feel completely
enthusiastic. It is indeed remarkable that it should have
realised a quarter as much again as any other picture in the
famous Slingeland sale of 1785. It is possible that it reminded
the French dealers (for some reason the British were not
represented) of their favourite Wouwermans. The church in
the background is based on the Marekerk at Utrecht. The exact
meaning of the statues and the broken pediments in the
foreground is obscure.

136 River landscape, huntsmen and peasants
canvas $46\frac{1}{2} \times 67$in./117×167 cm., inscribed *A. cuyp*
National Gallery of Art, Washington (Widener Collection)
first recorded collection J. van der Linden van Slingeland 1752
painted late 1650s; reference HdG 430

This and R135 hung as pendants in the Slingeland collection
but, as has already been said in relation to R104 and 106,
this does not necessarily imply that they were originally
painted as such. Though their style is similar, the two
paintings do not really match; this perhaps explains why
their common background has so long been overlooked.

137 Horseman in a red cloak, mountainous landscape
canvas 52 × 81in./132 × 206cm., inscribed *A. cuyp*
National Trust, Waddesdon Manor
first recorded collection W. Stratford Dugdale 1880
painted late 1650s; reference HdG 458a and 711

A somewhat eclectic work which seems, fundamentally, to lack
sufficient justification for a picture of so large a size. Certain
details recall R135.

138 Peasants near a river
canvas $44\frac{1}{2} \times 66$in./111×165cm.
Dulwich College Picture Gallery, London
first recorded Desenfans sale 1801
painted mid 1650s; reference HdG 435

A superlative painting of Cuyp's penultimate period, with the
most beautiful autumnal colouring.

139 Cavaliers watering their steeds
canvas 51 × 91in./129 × 227cm., inscribed *A. cuyp*
Rijksmuseum, Amsterdam
first recorded collection Desenfans 1796
painted late 1650s; reference HdG 458
reproduced in colour, plate X

By any standards one of the best half dozen paintings by the
artist, others being R98, 103, 104, 124 and 140. A fine
associated drawing is in a private collection in London.

140 River landscape with horseman and peasants
canvas 49 × 96½in./123 × 241cm., inscribed *A. cuyp*
The Marquess of Bute
first recorded collection Earl of Bute 1764
painted late 1650s; reference HdG 433
reproduced in colour, plate XI

With the exception of the equestrian piece in the Washington
Gallery (R124), this picture is in a style clearly later than that
of all other paintings by Cuyp. It is so perfectly wrought that
it is almost understandable he should have felt inhibited from
proceeding further. The condition of the painting is faultless
apart from the very regrettable loss of some ten inches of sky.
The engraving by T. Elliot, made in 1764 when the picture
was already in the possession of an ancestor of the present
owner, gives the measurements as 60 × 96 inches (150 × 240cm.).

The influence of Aelbert Cuyp

141 Portrait group, landscape background
canvas 67 × 96in./168 × 240cm., inscribed *A. cuyp fecit*
Museum of Fine Arts, Budapest
first recorded Schwanberg sale, Paris 1809
Studio of Aelbert Cuyp early 1650s; reference HdG 84 and 98

The costume shows that this curious picture was probably
painted sometime between 1648 and 1652. According to the
Schwanberg catalogue it represents the Thiboel family of
Dordrecht, with Heidelberg in the background, but no family
of this name has yet been traced. The style may be compared
with that of the portraits of Grootebroeck at Amsterdam
(HdG 81) and Pieter de Roovere at The Hague (HdG 42).
In reality such pictures (HdG 159 is another) may well have
been painted in the studio of J. G. Cuyp at a time when
Aelbert's influence was already in the ascendant; it is also
likely that they are the work of a collaboration.

142 Ships in a storm
canvas 43 × 59in./107 × 147cm., inscribed *A.C.*
The Louvre, Paris
first recorded J. van der Linden van Slingeland sale 1785
School of Aelbert Cuyp early 1660s
reference HdG 643 and 650

This painting directly derives from R101 and R102. On the
right can be seen the Kil Guard-house before the land around
it was re-claimed in the middle 1660s (see note to R146).

143 Landscape with cattle and figures
canvas $53 \times 78\frac{1}{2}$in./135×201cm., inscribed *A. cuyp*
National Gallery, London (by courtesy of the Trustees)
first recorded Sir Lawrence Dundas sale 1794
Studio of Aelbert Cuyp early 1660s; reference HdG 426

This picture has undeniable qualities and, had it been possible
to give it a date earlier in the painter's career, acceptance
would not have been so difficult. But iconological factors
point strongly towards the 1660s, by which time – if he was
still painting – Cuyp's style was already highly formal and
sophisticated (*cf*. R124 and R140). More than any other
painting it seems to stand on the borderline between Cuyp and
his imitators, and possesses a certain geniality which has not
previously been so clearly marked. On the other hand, the
structure is weak, facile and inconsistent.

144 Rhineland landscape, herdsmen and cattle
canvas 52 × 72in./130 × 180cm., inscribed *A. cuyp*
Lord Scarsdale, Kedleston Hall
first recorded Dr Bragge sale 1759
Studio of Aelbert Cuyp early 1660s; reference HdG 425

Very similar to the previous painting: diffuse, eclectic, soft,
pink, yet not without distinction. It is possible the horseman
is intended as a portrait and that it is Cuyp himself who is
represented. The rider is also seen full face in a second version
of the same subject (HdG 437). The features closely resemble
those of the model who sat for Orpheus in R48.

145 Landscape with herdsman drawing water
canvas $44\frac{1}{2} \times 69\frac{1}{2}$in./$111 \times 174$cm.
National Trust, Petworth
first recorded Sir Philip Stephens sale 1810
Follower of Aelbert Cuyp; reference HdG 337 and 444

Another work of exceptional quality but lacking the hard
brilliance of Cuyp's characteristic late style and unusually
cold in tone. It would be easier to discuss its authorship if
some comparable painting were known. It is slightly reminiscent
of Frederick de Moucheron (1633–86) but there is no evidence
that he or any other Italianiser was even aware of Cuyp's
existence.

146 A yacht near the Kil guard–house
canvas $41\frac{1}{2} \times 78$in./104×195cm., inscribed *A. cuyp*
London sale, 27 November 1963
first recorded collection Sir Lawrence Dundas 1781
Follower of Aelbert Cuyp late 1660s.

Dr Horst Gerson has argued (*Opus musivum: Feestbundel
voor Prof. Dr M. D. Ozinga,* 1964, p. 257 ff) that the building
seen on the left is the former guard-house on the canal
connecting the Maas with the Hollandsch Diep, and that, as
the land around it was not re-claimed until the mid 1660s,
the picture cannot have been painted before 1665. It is not
only for this reason, however, that Cuyp's authorship is
rejected. Once again, despite great qualities, it simply does not
stand comparison with its prototype: R99. The guard-house,
or ferry-house as it is sometimes called, is seen before the
reclamation in R142, and in its later state in HdG 166 and
167 (R147). If Dr Gerson's analysis is correct, these pictures
provide an invaluable starting point for the study of Cuyp's
later following. One curious feature is the fact that the figures
in the yacht wear the costume of the late 1640s.

147 The old ferry–house, Dordrecht
panel 14×20in./35×50cm.
Present whereabouts unknown
first recorded collection Duc de Choiseuil 1772
reference HdG 167

148 Prince Frederick Henry at Heusden
panel $19\frac{1}{2} \times 23\frac{1}{2}$in./$48 \times 59$cm.
Tritsch sale, April 1933
first recorded J. van der Linden van Slingeland sale 1785
School of Aelbert Cuyp; reference HdG 27

This and the succeeding three paintings are typical of those
now ascribed to Abraham van Calraet despite their
distinguished pedigrees. The exploits of Frederick Henry
seem to have been among the specialities of the Cuyp
workshop. It has been suggested that the town is Bouvignes
and not Heusden.

149 Prince Frederick Henry at Dordrecht
panel 15×23in./38×58cm.
London sale, 29 October 1941
first recorded probably H. van der Vugt sale 1745
School of Aelbert Cuyp; reference HdG 36a and 36b

An undistinguished pastiche based on R104 and R106. The
van der Vught sale catalogue correctly identified the subject
but not the artist.

150 Grooms watering their horses

copper 18×21in./45×53cm., inscribed *A.C.*
Rikoff sale, Paris 1907
first recorded J. van der Linden van Slingeland sale 1785
School of Aelbert Cuyp; reference HdG 40 and 595

It is remarkable that this picture – in relation to its size –
realised a higher price in the Slingeland sale of 1785 than,
for instance, Cuyp's classic river scene in the Washington
gallery (R104). The catalogue rightly draws attention to the
influence of Wouwermans, at the time the favourite painter in
France and Holland.

151 Winter scene, Dordrecht

panel 13½×22½in./33×57cm., inscribed *A.C.*
National Gallery, London (by courtesy of the Trustees)
first recorded J. van der Linden van Slingeland sale 1785
School of Aelbert Cuyp; reference HdG 735 and 739

Another of the thirty-eight pictures sold with the Slingeland
collection in 1785 (*see* p. 212) but given a lower valuation
than R148 and 150: an assessment which would still be
considered valid.

152 River scene with horseman, peasants and cattle
canvas 43 × 62in./107 × 155cm.
Private collection, London
first recorded collection J. van der Linden van Slingeland 1785
Follower of Aelbert Cuyp; reference HdG 226 and 454

One of the highest priced 'Cuyps' in the Slingeland sale and
much vaunted throughout the nineteenth century, this picture
now appears lifeless and flat, somewhat in the taste of Johannes
Glauber (1646–*circa* 1726) and Jacob de Heusch (1657–1701).
As unfortunately no photograph is available, it is here
represented by a drawing made by George Scarf at the time
of the great Manchester exhibition in 1857. The famous
moonlight scene in the Six collection (HdG 719) is slightly
similar in style.

153 Rhineland landscape with horsemen and peasants
panel 16½ × 22in./41 × 55cm.
De Rothschild, Paris
first recorded collection Baron Denon 1826
Follower of Albert Cuyp; reference HdG 449

Another painting, much praised in the past, which now seems
too soft for Cuyp. The lithograph was apparently made at
about the time of the Denon sale in 1826. There is a
somewhat similar painting, agreeable but insipid, in the
Dulwich Gallery (HdG 434).

154 Cows with milkmaid and sleeping herdsman

canvas $51\frac{1}{2}\times67\frac{1}{2}$in./$129\times168$cm., inscribed *A. cuyp*
Art trade, 1958
first recorded Grand-Pré sale 1809
Cuyp forgery *circa* 1800; reference HdG 343

In 1809, this grotesque picture established the record Cuyp auction price of 30,000 francs (£1,300). A vast number of 'Cuyps' were forged between 1770 and 1810; this is a particularly crude example.

155 Cavalier on a grey horse

canvas approximately 26×32in./65×80cm.
Nazi looted property, Munich 1947
first recorded collection Brown (picture-cleaner) 1839
Cuyp follower unknown date; reference HdG 457

This picture fetched the astonishing price of £5,040 in 1876, considerably more than any other painting of corresponding size apart from R119. Smith also wrote in rapturous terms in 1842: 'an example of the highest excellence, offering a rich display of the golden hues and magic tints of this painter's unrivalled palette.' Without having seen the picture, it is difficult to deny these claims with conviction. The composition does, however, appear weak and confused. It is a little surprising that so small a picture should be on canvas; possibly it was once a little larger. There are points of comparison with R137 as well as HdG 434. Probably a school piece rather than a forgery.

Appendices

Appendix A:
ARNOLD HOUBRAKEN

The account of Aelbert Cuyp given in the first volume of Houbraken's *De Groote Schouburgh der Nederlantsche Konstschilders en Schilderessen*, published in 1718, provides the sole source of information about the painter's work apart from the paintings themselves. As Houbraken was himself born in Dordrecht in 1660, and spent most of his early life there, he must have known the artist personally. Yet he tells us very little and we are left with the strong impression that Cuyp had long ceased to be active as a painter by the time Houbraken's own career began.

The account is preceded by a brief statement concerning Jacob Gerritsz Cuyp and in volume III, published posthumously in 1721, the biographer also mentions Bastian van der Leeuw and the two brothers van Calraet, Abraham and Barent. The relevant passages are here reproduced in Dutch and English.

Volume I page 237: **Jacob Gerritszoon Cuyp**

Wy hadden byna vergeten den braven Dordrechtse Konstschilder JAKOB GERRETZE KUIP, *wiens penceelkonst al vroeg de konstminnende bekoord heeft, te gedenken; maar wierden hem indagtig als wy zyn Zoon Albert Kuip ten Toneel zoude voeren. Hy schilderden Osjes, Koetjes, Schaapjes enz. De verschieten agter de zelve waren meest land – en watergezigten die zig om en by Dord doen zien, welke hy tot zyn gebruik naar 't leven afgeteekent heeft, en zyn wyze van schilderen was helder gloeijend en smeltende.*

Zeze JAKOB GERRETZE KUIP, *Dortenaar, leerling van* Abr. Bloemaert, IZAK VAN HASSELT, KORN. TEGELBERG *beide landschapschilders, en* JAQUES GRIEF, *anders Klaau, die stil leven schilderde, waren de hoofden of aanleiders welke in den jare 1642 het konstgenootschap van St. Lukas te Dordrecht hebben opgeregt, na dat zy uit het Gild, genoemt het Gild van de vyf Neringen (Volgens deding als in de Acte van scheiding staat uitgedrukt) waren uitgegaan.*

We had almost forgotten the worthy Dordrecht painter JAKOB GERRETZE KUIP, whose work at an early stage enchanted art lovers; but we remembered him as we were about to present his son Albert Kuip. He painted Oxen, Cows, Sheep, etc. As a background he mainly used the land and water scenery around Dordrecht, which he drew from nature as was his wont, and his manner of painting was richly glowing and well blended.

This JAKOB GERRETZE KUIP, of Dordrecht, pupil of *Abr. Bloemaert*, IZAK VAN HASSELT, KORN. TEGELBERG, both landscape painters, and JAQUES GRIEF, otherwise known as *Klaau*, who painted still life, were the prime movers in establishing the brotherhood of St. Luke in Dordrecht in 1642, after they had left the Guild of the five Trades (on account of a disagreement according to the Deed of separation).

Volume I page 248: **Aelbert Cuyp**

AALBERT KUIP *geboren te Dordrecht in 't jaar 1605. Deze was den zoon van* JAKOB GERRITZE KUIP, *een braaf schilder, by wien hy de Konst geleerd heeft, hoe wel hy in handeling veel van zyn Vader verscheelde; want hy wat meer aan den netten kant was: ook zoo ruw in zyne penceelbehandeling niet als zyn Neef* BENJAMIN KUIP *die een medeleerling met hem was; hoewel ik 'er dingen van gezien heb, die meesterlyk aangetoetst waren. Daarenboven hield zig zyn Vader aan eenerhande vierkiezinge. Hem daarentegen scheen het evenveel te*

wezen wat hy ook maakte. Ossen, Koeijen, Schapen, Schapen, Paerden, Fruit, Landschap, stil water met Scheepen; 't scheen hem alles onverschillig te wezen, en daar men zig over verwonderen moet, is, dat hy alles even fraai en natuurlyk schilderde. Daarenboven heeft hy inzonderheid wel in agt genomen de tydstonden waar in hy de voorwerpen verbeelde, zoo dat men den benevelden morgenstond van den klaren middag, en dezen weer van den saffraan-werwigen avonstond in zyn tafereelen kost onderscheiden. Ook heb ik verscheide maanligten van hem gezien die heel natuurlyk verbeeld waren, en zoo geschikt dat dezelve een aangename spiegeling in 't water maakten. Onder zyne Konststukken zyn wel de voornamste, daar hy de Dordsche Beestemarkt in verbeeld, als ook de Pikeurbaan, daar hy dan de schilderagtigste Paerden die daar gewoonlyk kwamen, in te pas bragt, zoo dat men dezelve kost onderkennen. Dat 'er na zyn dood geen modellen of teekenen van andere meesters by hem gevonden wierden is een bewys dat hy alleen de natuur tot leiding nam. 't Was ook zyn aart niet geld daar ann te besteenden, want hy had altyd tot zinspreuk: In harde Ryksdaalders komt de mot niet. Egter was hy een man van onbesproken leven, en ouderling van de Gereformeerde Kerk.

Hy heeft in zyn tyd menigte van landschapgezigten zoo buiten Dordrecht als elders getekend, die met zwart kryt omgetrokken, en met sapjes opgewasschen, geestig en natuurlyk behandelt zyn.

AALBERT KUIP was born at Dordrecht in the year 1605. He was the son of JAKOB GERRITZE KUIP, a worthy painter from whom he learnt the art, although his handling was quite different from that of his father, in that he was much more precise: nor was his brushwork as rough as that of his cousin BENJAMIN KUIP who was a fellow-apprentice of his; although I must admit that I have seen a few things by the latter which show a masterly touch. Moreover his father confined himself to one area of preference. To Aalbert, however, it seemed to make no difference what he painted. Oxen, Cows, Sheep, Horses, Fruit, Landscape, still water with Ships; they were all the same to him, and what is so remarkable is that he painted them all in a manner which was equally fine and natural. Moreover he paid much attention to the time of day in which he portrayed his subjects, so that one can distinguish in his paintings the misty early morning from the bright afternoon and that again from the saffron-coloured evening-time. I have also seen various moonlight scenes by him which were very realistic and arranged in such a way that the moon was beautifully reflected in the water. Among his most notable works of art are those which depict the

Dordrecht Cattle Market, and also the Riding School, where the most lively horses often came to be broken in, so that each one could be recognized. The fact that no work by other masters was found at his home after his death proves that only nature served as his model. Anyway, it was not like him to spend money on such things, for his life-long motto was: *Hard coins are not attacked by the moth.* However, he was a man of blameless character, an elder of the Calvinist Church.

In his time he made many landscape-studies of the area around Dordrecht and elsewhere, which he sketched in outline with black crayon and tinted with watercolours and executed in a spirited and lifelike manner.

Volume III page 179: **Bastian Govertszoon van der Leeuw**

GABRIEL *vander* LEEUW, *anders* De Lione, *is geboren te Dordrecht, op den 11 van Slachtmaant 1643. Zyn vader Bastiaan Govertz vander Leeuw, was een fraai schilder van Osjes, Koetjes, Schaapjes enz. Leerling van Jacob Gerritz Kuip, dog verwisselde naderhand het penceel, voor de* Collecte *van de Bieren te Dordrecht.*

GABRIEL, *al vroeg, door het voorbeeld van zyn Vader, tot de Konst aangespoort, draafde in weinig jaren zny Vader vooruit in de penceel-oeffening, zoo dat hy al vroeg berucht wierd.*

GABRIEL vander LEEUW, otherwise known as *De Lione*, was born at Dordrecht, on the 11th of November 1643. His father Bastiaan Govertz vander Leeuw was a fine painter of oxen, cows, sheep, etc. Pupil of Jacob Gerritz Kuip, he afterwards exchanged the paint brush for trading in beer in Dordrecht.

GABRIEL, at an early age, following the example of his father, addressed himself to the Art, advancing so rapidly that in a few years he surpassed his father in the technique of painting, with the result that he very soon became famous.

Volume III page 181: **Abraham van Calraet**

ABRAHAM van KALRAAT, *geboren te Dordrecht, in't jaar 1643 den 7 van Wynmaant, heeft de gronden van de Teekenkonst geleert by Aemilius en Samuel Hup. of Huppe, beroemde Steen-Beeldhouwers.*

ABRAHAM, *door yver en vlyt, heeft na dien tyd, zig tot penceel begeven, en oeffende zig op beelden en fruit; en alzoo zyn Vader, die een houtbeeldhouwer was, door ouderdom afviel, hanteerde hy ook den beitel. Hy is thans nog in leven, en oeffent de Schilderkonst en Beeldhouwery.*

ABRAHAM van KALRAAT, born in Dordrecht in the year 1643 on the 7th of October, learnt the groundings of draughtmanship from Aemilius and Samuel Hup, or Huppe, well-known sculptors.

ABRAHAM, through zeal and diligence, in due course acquired mastery of the paint brush, and practised both sculpture and the painting of fruit; as also his Father, who was a woodcarver, needed assistance in his old age, he likewise handled the chisel. He is still living, and practises both painting and sculpture.

Volume III page 292: **Barent van Calraet**

BARENT *van* KALRAAT *geboren te Dordrecht in den jare 1650 den 28 Augustus, heeft tot onderwyzer in de teekenkonst van zyn 12 jaar tot zyn 15 jaar zyn Broeder Abraham gehad. Daar na bestelde hem zyn Vader by Albert Kuip, zoon van Jakob Gerritsz. Kuip, waar van wy hier boven gemelt hebben. Albert Kuip die zig wel't best op't schilderen van paarden in't kleen verstont, heeft hy nagebootst, maar gelyk de menschen (als het spreekwoort zeit) by verandering leven, zoo heeft hy zig naderhand gezet op't schilderen van Rhyngezigten, op de wys van Herman Zachtleven, die hy al vry na op't spoor wist te volgen. Hy oeffent zig nog dagelyks in de Konst, schoon hy (onder't zeiltje is't goed roejen, zeit het spreekwoort) een andere kost-winning aan de hand heeft.*

BARENT van KALRAAT, born at Dordrecht on the 28th of August 1650, was taught the art of drawing by his brother Abraham between 12 and 15 years of age. Then his father apprenticed him to Albert Kuip, son of Jakob Gerritsz Kuip, whom we mentioned earlier. He imitated Albert Kuip, specializing in painting horses on a small scale, but as the proverb says: variety is the spice of life, and so afterwards he turned to Rhine-views, in the manner of Herman Zachtleven whom he soon managed to imitate quite closely. He still paints every day, although he also makes a living by other means (as the proverb says: with the sail hoisted, it is easy rowing).

Pastoral scene by J. G. Cuyp.
This picture, which is signed and dated 1627 and was formerly in the Nesselrode collection (more recently with D. Katz of Dieren), probably represents Aelbert with his mother, Aertjen van Cooten. He would have been 6 or 7 years old at the time. There is a similar picture in the Rijksmuseum, Amsterdam, dated 1628.

Two writers have attempted comprehensive catalogues of the works of Aelbert Cuyp: John Smith in 1834 (with supplement in 1842) and Hofstede de Groot in 1908 (English edition in 1909). As de Groot included every picture listed by Smith, as well as many others, it is to his catalogue that reference is invariably made. On the other hand, Smith's appreciation of the painter appears in many ways the more perceptive and he made few mistakes in his approach to the work of Cuyp's maturity. It was only in his interpretation of the artist's early period that he was seriously wide of the mark, ascribing to the beginnings of Cuyp's career many paintings which are now seen to be the work of imitators.

It must be realized that both writers – de Groot to a far greater extent than Smith – listed numerous works they knew only from unreliable sale catalogue descriptions, and it is not surprising that the great majority of these have never come to light. In most cases they have disappeared simply because they were works of no significance.

In the accompanying table, the pictures described by Smith are classified according to three categories: those illustrated in the present book, those not reproduced but nevertheless identifiable (code letter I), and those which have apparently been lost. Where the painting can still be recognized, its last known location may be found by referring to the corresponding number in the Hofstede de Groot (HdG) table in Appendix C.

Comparative Table: John Smith

Smith	HdG	Reiss	
1	649	32	
2	652	I	
3	738	112	
4	229	I	= Sm 202
5	446a		
6	317	I	= Sm 41
7	325	88	= Sm 43
8	231	I	= Sm 203
9	473a	23	= Sup 32
10	430	136	
11	448	135	
12	30	103	
13	36	106	
14	650	142	
15	719	I	
16	246	I	= Sm 99
17	526	I	
18	491	I	
19	737	111	
20	454	152	
21	367	I	= Sm 70 and Sup 9
22	432	133	
23	495		
24	633	100	= Sup 10
25	639	102	= Sm 175
26	739	151	
27	465	46	= Sup 56
28	605	I	
29	450	I	
30	27	148	
31	39	I	
32	234	I	

Smith	HdG	Reiss	
33	380a		
34	418	I	
35	10b		
36	12	118	
37	651		
38	726		
39	341	I	
40	448a	I	= Sm 221
41	236	I	= Sm 6
42	736	I	
43	325	88	= Sm 7
44	619		
45	235c		
46	237		
47	780a		
48	235d		
49	235e		
50	566a		
51	567		
52	426	143	
53	760		
54	345	I	
55	354		
56	355		
57	389	39	
58	235f		
59	236a	134	
60	237c		
61	399		
62	170	I	
63	237f		
64	237d		

Smith	HdG	Reiss	
65	237e	44	
66	527	117	= Sup 13
67	490	I	
68	113	I	
69	335	I	
70	367	I	= Sm 21 and Sup 9
71	723	I	= Sup 8
72	435	138	
73	201	I	
74	318		
75	203	92	
76	238a		
77	239	15	
78	765		
79	240		
80	330	44	
81	315	I	= Sm 248
82	712g		
83	467	I	= Sm 261
84	358		
85	727	34	
86	241a		
87	244		
88	245		
89	658	107	
90	410	I	
91	437	I	
92	425	144	
93	424	89	
94	259	64	
95	448d		
96	657		
97	679	I	
98	28	104	
99	247	I	= Sm 16
100	242		? = Sm 80
101	653		
102	427	I	
103	350	I	
104	245a	I	
105	477	I	
106	407	I	
107	624e		
108	343	154	
109	342	79	= Sm 208
110	246a		
111	246b		
112	549	113	
113	337	145	
114	402		
115	168	119	= Sup 23
116	53	I	
117	780b		
118	176	132	
119	775	I	
120	438	I	
121	782		
122	198	74	
123	401		
124	74	70	
125	339	I	
126	419	71	
127	783		
128	784		
129	766		
130	436		= Sm 189 and Sup 28
131	546	I	
132	409	I	
133	747		
134	172	40	
135	267		
136	218		
137	655		
138	415	137	= Sup 47
139	512d		
140	480		
141	193	126	
142	338	I	
143	249	29	
144	522		
145	25	I	= Sup 24
146	523	I	= Sm 270
147	260	I	
148	525a	I	
149	206	I	
150	617	121	
151	72	120	
152	767	I	
153	773	I	
154	65	I	
155	627	122	
156	468		
157	413		
158	359	58	

Smith	HdG	Reiss	
159	340	I	
160	600	I	
161	733	112	
162	310	I	
163	40	150	
164	391	88	
165	180	I	= Sup 25
166	763		
167	810		
168	525		
169	98	141	
170	390	85	
171	641	110	
172	724	77	
173	209	I	
174	616	I	
175	639	102	= Sm 25
176	109	I	
177	618	124	= Sup 48
178	50	I	
179	363	I	= Sup 26
180	302	82	= Sm 183
181	175	127	
182	73	I	
183	230	82	= Sm 180
184	762	I	
185	497		
186	449	153	
187	164	98	= Sup 52
188	164	98	= Sup 52
189	436		= Sm 130 and Sup 28
190	261		
191	509	I	
192	596		
193	631	97	= Sup 29
194	452	I	= Sup 15
195	186	72	= Sup 16
196	19	48	
197	392	I	
198	349	I	
199	394	78	= Sup 17
200	34	93	
201	659e	109	
202	202	I	= Sm 4
203	263	I	= Sm 8
204	489	I	
205	208	I	

Smith	HdG	Reiss	
206	116		
207	227	76	
208	342	79	= Sm 109
209	768		
210	560	I	= Sup 30
211	512	I	
212	744	I	
213	506	I	
214	422	I	
215	585	I	
216	31	105	
217	573	I	
218	537		
219	531	I	
220	580		
221	420	I	= Sm 40
222	393	86	
223	205	I	
224	32	95	
225	369	56	
226	329	I	
227	501	I	
228	646	I	
229	507	I	
230	621	I	= Sup 34
231	(378)	I	see R91
232	410e		
233	449c		
234	262		
235	591	I	
236	5	I	= Sup 7
237	599		
238	137	I	
239	423	131	
240	264	73	
241	550	114	
242	200	II	
243	370	I	
244	488	116	
245	500	I	
246	818	I	
247	637	99	
248	183	I	= Sm 81
249	612	I	
250	730	75	
251	529	I	
252	414		

Smith	HdG	Reiss	
253	326	I	
254	405		
255	659	I	
256	37	I	
257	528		
258	319	I	= Sup 42
259	332	84	
260	174	128	
261	434	I	= Sm 83
262	446	90	
263	652a		
264	433	140	
265	24	I	
266	808	I	
267	558	I	
268	70	I	
269	713	I	
270	539	I	= Sm 146
271	515	I	
272	832		
273	833		
274	248e		
275	486		
276	487		
277	372	I	
278	272	I	
279	740	I	
280	184	I	
S1	563	I	
S2	645	I	
S3	379	57	
S4	395	I	
S5	396	87	
S6	644	I	
S7	5	I	= Sm 236
S8	723	I	= Sm 71
S9	367	I	= Sm 21 and 70
S10	640	96	= Sm 24
S11	406	37	
S12	457	155	
S13	527	117	= Sm 66
S14	263	I	= Sm 203
S15	452	I	= Sm 194
S16	270	72	= Sm 195
S17	394	78	= Sm 199
S18	77	I	
S19	502	I	

Smith	HdG	Reiss	
S20	786a		
S21	698		
S22	26	I	
S23	168	119	= Sm 115
S24	25	I	= Sm 145
S25	180	I	= Sm 165
S26	363	I	= Sm 179
S27	291	I	
S28	436		= Sm 130
S29	631	97	= Sm 193
S30	560	I	= Sm 210
S31	585	I	= Sm 215
S32	473	23	= Sm 9
S33	510	I	cf. Sm 229
S34	621	I	= Sm 230
S35	458	139	
S36	626	I	
S37	552	I	
S38	534	I	
S39	213	I	
S40	451		
S41	159	I	
S42	319	I	= Sm 258
S43	574		
S44	36b	149	
S45	327	81	
S46	654	I	
S47	415	137	= Sm 138
S48	618	124	= Sm 177
S49	81	I	
S50	384	I	
S51	376	I	
S52	164	98	= Sm 187
S53	533		
S54	787		
S55	206	I	
S56	465	46	= Sm 27
S57	61	I	
S58	530b		
S59	374	43	

Appendix C : HOFSTEDE DE GROOT

When Hofstede de Groot published his catalogue in 1908, he listed sixteen hundred pictures. At the time, it was possible to trace about three hundred and seventy. Another fifty have since come to light but the remaining twelve hundred are probably best forgotten; some – inadequately described – may well have reappeared without the earlier reference being recognized, but in the vast majority of cases it is clear the pictures were either valueless or have subsequently been re-named; further search would thus be futile. The accompanying table lists only those which can be located or identified from reproductions to be found in one of the major photographic libraries, such as the Witt in London or the Rijksbureau voor Kunsthistorische Documentatie at The Hague.

It might have been helpful to refer to those pictures which, since the publication of de Groot's catalogue, have been re-attributed to other artists. But it was felt that by doing so an arbitrary and misleading distinction would be drawn between these pictures and numerous others which, though similar in style, have not as yet been re-named. Moreover, many of the new attributions are no more than tentative and much further research is needed before they can be confirmed. This applies particularly in the case of Abraham van Calraet who has simply become a convenient dumping ground for anything which is clearly sub-Cuyp. In 1926, de Groot himself attempted a reconstruction of this artist's oeuvre solely by reference to his own Cuyp catalogue (Thieme-Becker *Künstler Lexikon* XIX) but his opinions in this context are unfortunately no more reliable than those he had previously advanced.

Since the publication of de Groot's catalogue, about fifteen pictures have come to light which he had apparently failed to record. With one exception (R129), however, they all belong to the artist's early period. The chances of finding an undocumented work of Cuyp's maturity cannot be rated very high, nor can there be more than one or two, which, though listed, have long escaped attention. On the other hand, there may well be several paintings of his early time which have yet to be discovered.

HdG	Smith	Reiss	Last known collection	Other notes
1			Basel	
2			Paris dealer 1908	
5	236		Amsterdam sale 1926	
8			New York sale 8 July 1927	= HdG 442
9			Glasgow	
10			Dr. Wetzlar	
11	36	118	Anglesey Abbey (NT)	= HdG 12
11a		6	De Menil, Houston	
12			= HdG 11	
16			London dealer 1950's	
18		5	Dessau	
19	196	48	Marquess of Bute	
22			Wroclaw	
23			Royal collection, Holland	
24	265		Northbrook 1889	
25	145		Lady Douglas Pennant	
26	S22		Massey-Mainwaring sale 19 June 1898	See HdG 27 (confused provenance)
27	30	148	Tritsch sale, Vienna, April 1933	
28	98	104	National Gallery, Washington	
29			Earl of Wemyss	
30	12	103	Duke of Sutherland	
31	216	105	Waddesdon Manor (NT)	= HdG 647
32	224	95	David Robarts	= HdG 32
33			= HdG 32	
34	200	93	Wallace Collection, London	= HdG 167b
36	13	106	Waddesdon Manor (NT)	
36b	S44	149	London sale 29 Oct. 1941	? = HdG 36a
36c			Duke of Buccleugh	
37	256		Paul Getty	
38			Amsterdam Rijksmuseum	
39	31		London sale 28 Mar. 1969	
40	163	150	Rikoff sale 4 Dec. 1907	= HdG 595
41			Schubart sale 1899	
42			The Hague Mauritshuis	
44			Cologne sale 1962	
46			London sale 8 Dec. 1961	
47			Hague dealer 1943	
48			Hague dealer 1943	
50	178		Rotterdam	See also London sale 14 Dec. 1962
52			London sale 29 Jan. 1966	
53	116		Klaasen, Rotterdam (1946)	

HdG	Smith	Reiss	Last known collection	Other notes	HdG	Smith	Reiss	Last known collection	Other notes
54			Paris sale 23 Mar. 1971		129			Douai Museum	
54a			London sale 18 Jul. 1930		132f			Paris sale 21 Nov. 1918	
57			Amsterdam Museum		133a			London sale 27 Feb. 1939	
58			Louisville, Kentucky		137	238		Bischoffsheim, Paris	
59b		125	London sale 12 Nov. 1934		138			Exhibited Brussels 1935	
					145			Mrs M. M. Fry	
61	S57		New York sale 17 Jan 1922	= HdG 436a, 450	146			Copenhagen Museum	
					148			Paris dealer 1908	
65	154		Art Museum, Ponce, U.S.A.		153			London sale 25 Nov. 1970	
					156			London sale 6 July 1917	
68			Dordrecht Folk Museum		157			Y Collection (1908)	
					158			Innsbruck	
69			St Omer		159	S41		London sale 23 Mar. 1973	
69a		17	Paula da Koenigsberg		160			Louvre, Paris	
70	268		E. de Rothschild		161			Private collection, England	J. G. Cuyp
71			Castle Howard						
72	151	120	Duke of Bedford		161a			Cologne	as J. G. Cuyp
73	182		Duke of Bedford		162			Amsterdam sale 19 Nov. 1929	as Donck
74	124	70	Strasbourg Museum	= HdG 78					
75		41	Krupp von Bohlen		163			Dordrecht	
77	S18		Brooklyn		164	S52	98	Ascott, Leighton Buzzard (NT)	
78			= HdG 74						
79			London sale 17 May 1961		165	193	97	Kenwood House, London	= HdG 631
81	S49		Amsterdam Rijksmuseum						
					166			Berlin	
84	169	141	Budapest	= HdG 98	167		147	Engraved Choiseul Collection	
85	150	121	New York Metropolitan	= HdG 617					
91			London sale 29 Oct. 1965		167b			= HdG 34	
94			S. Nystad, The Hague (1970)		167c		101	National Gallery, London	= HdG 636
97			Amiens		167d			London dealer 1960s	
98			= HdG 84		168	115	119	Wallace Collection, London	
99			New York dealer 1920						
101			R. von Schnitzler, Cologne (1931)		169			Mrs J. Salmond, Malmesbury	
104			London sale 7 Mar. 1930 as Bol		170	62		Duke of Sutherland	
109	176		National Gallery, London		171			Duke of Sutherland	
					172	134	40	Montpellier	
110a			London sale 8 Apr. 1938		173	260	128	Edinburgh	= HdG 174
111			London sale 13 Jul. 1923		174			= HdG 173	
113	68		Louvre, Paris		175	181	127	Duke of Bedford	= HdG 175b
115			A. Schloss (1908)		175b			= HdG 175	
117			Exhibited Brussels 1935		176	118	132	National Gallery, London	
125			De Boer, Amsterdam (1937)		177			Rotterdam	
126			Fursac, Brussels, 1923		179			London dealer 1922	
128			Dordrecht	as J. G. Cuyp	180	165		Amsterdam	

HdG	Smith	Reiss	Last known collection	Other notes
181	162		Art trade 1908	= HdG 310
182			Munich	
183	248		Duke of Rutland	= HdG 315
184	280		Cologne	
185			Thyssen, Lugano	
186	195	72	Mrs M. M. Fry	= HdG 270
187			Leinster sale 14 May 1926	
188			Wernher, Luton Hoo	
189			London sale 1 Apr. 1960	
191	203		Private collection, Dorset	= HdG 231, 263, 291a
193	141	126	Frankfurt	
194	41		Sir Edmund Bacon	= HdG 236, 317
195	278		Glasgow	= HdG 272
196		130	Indianapolis	
197			Hopetoun House, Scotland	
198	122	74	B. de Geus van den Heuvel	
199	32		Lille Museum	= HdG 234
200	242		Buckingham Palace, London	
201	73		Dulwich College	
201a		80	Dulwich College	
202	202		Lord Iveagh (1938)	= HdG 229
203	75	92	National Gallery, Washington	
204	142		Morrison family	= HdG 338, 464
205	223		David Robarts	
206	149		National Gallery, London	
207	16		Wallace Collection, London	= HdG 246, 247
208	205		Wallace Collection, London	
209	173		Duke of Westminster (1908)	
210			Horne, Montreal (1933)	
211			New York	
212	180	82	Frick Collection, New York	= HdG 302, possibly 230
213	S39		Petit Palais, Paris	
214			Antwerp sale 1898	
215			Geldner, Basel	
216	158	58	Sarasota	= HdG 359, 383b
217			New York Metropolitan	
218	136		Paris dealer 1908	Confused provenance
219		(10)	Paris sale 2 Jun. 1924	= HdG 687, see R10
220			Art trade 1960s	
221			Count Bloudoff (1908)	
222			Philadelphia	
223			Prague	
224			London sale 25 Nov. 1966	? = HdG 245a, 265
226	20	152	Private collection, London	= HdG 454
227	207	76	Residenz-Galerie, Salzburg	
228b		7	Lady Agnew, Melbury Park	= HdG 699
229	4		= HdG 202	
230	183		Compare HdG 212, 302	
230a		45	Mrs J. Salmond, Malmesbury	
231	8		= HdG 191, 263, 291a	
234	32		= HdG 199	
236	41		= HdG 194, 317	
236a	59	134	London sale 29 June 1973	= HdG 415
237e	65	44	Dulwich College	= HdG 330
239	77	15	Dulwich College	= HdG 697
243			A. Petschek, New York	
245a	104		= HdG 224, 265	or possibly replicas
246	16		= HdG 207	
247	99		= HdG 207	
249	143	29	Los Angeles	
259	94	64	Amsterdam sale 1971	= HdG 709
260	147		Polesden Lacy (NT)	
263	203		= HdG 191, 231, 291a	
264	240	73	Earl of Harrowby	
265			= HdG 224, 245a	or possibly replicas
268e		83	National Gallery, London	= HdG 368
270	S16		= HdG 186	
272	278		Glasgow	= HdG 195
275			Stitching Nederlands Kunstbezit	

HdG	Smith	Reiss	Last known collection	Other notes
288			Exhibited Copenhagen 1920	
291	S27		Ascott, Leighton Buzzard (NT)	
291a			= HdG 191, 231, 263	
295			London sale 29 Feb. 1956	
302	180		= HdG 212, and possibly 230	
302a			Walker Gallery, Minneapolis	
304			London sale 12 Nov. 1969	
310	162		= HdG 181	
312			Art trade, London, 1969	
313			Sedelmeyer 1907	
314			Berlin sale 1918	
315	81		= HdG 183	
316			Dijon	
317			= HdG 194, 236	
319	258		Detroit Art Institute	
322	253		Paris sale 1952	= HdG 326
323	S45	81	Baron de Rothschild, Paris	= HdG 327
325	43	88	National Gallery, London	= HdG 328, 391
326	253		= HdG 322	
327	S45		= HdG 323	
328	164		= HdG 325, 391	
329	226		Duke of Sutherland	
330	80		= HdG 237e	
331		51	New York, Metropolitan	
332	259	84	Louvre, Paris	
335	69		Cincinatti	
337	113	145	Petworth (NT)	= HdG 444
338	142		= HdG 204, 464	
339	125		Baron Thyssen, Lugano	
340	159		Art trade, London, 1950s	
341	39		Marquis d'Aoust (1908)	
342	109	79	National Gallery, London	
343	108	154	Exhibited Munich 1958	
345	54		David Robarts	= HdG 438
348			Private collection, Sweden	= HdG 360
349	198		Marquess of Bute	
350	103		Dulwich College	
353		54	Mainz	= HdG 557
359	158		= HdG 216	
360			= HdG 348	
361		61	J. Johnson, Philadelphia	
362		1	Besançon	
363	179		London sale 22 May 1925	
364		55	Dublin	
365			Glasgow	
366			Earl of Wemyss	
367	21		Art trade 1967 (ex Robit)	Confused provenance
367			Art trade 1956 (ex Weber)	Confused provenance
368			= HdG 268e	
369	225	56	Duke of Sutherland	
370	243		Buckingham Palace	
371			Dulwich College	
372	277		The Hague Mauritshuis	
373			Lord Crawford	
374	S59	43	Slatter exhibition 1952	
375			Private collection, America	= HdG 377
376	S51		New York sale 15 Feb. 1973	
377			= HdG 375	
378		91	Washington University, St Louis	not Smith 231
379	S3	57	Leningrad	
380b			Brooklyn	= HdG 387g
384	S50		Rotterdam	see R78
385			Timken Gallery, San Diego	see R78
387b			Detroit	
387g			= HdG 380b	
388			Berlin	
389	57	39	Stichting Nederlands Kunstbezit	= HdG 398
390	170	85	Budapest	
391	164		= 325, 328	
392	197		Marquess of Bute	
393	222	86	David Robarts	
394	199	78	Schloss 1908	
395	S4		Moscow	
396	S5	87	Leningrad	
397		108	Rotterdam	
398	57		= HdG 389	

HdG	Smith	Reiss	Last known collection	Other notes
406	S11	37	Amsterdam Rijksmuseum	
407	106		Amsterdam Rijksmuseum	
408			Lost in Berlin fire 1945	
409	132		London sale 28th June 1974	
410	90		Duke of Westminster 1908	
412		35	London sale 28 May 1937	
415	138		= HdG 236a	
416			New York sale 15 Apr. 1953	
417	126	71	Waddesdon Manor (NT)	= HdG 419
418	34		Baron Thyssen, Lugano	
419	126		= HdG 417	
420	221		E. de Rothschild, Ascott	= HdG 448a
421			Dordrecht	
422	214		Dordrecht	
423	239	131	Cardiff Museum	
424	93	89	Corcoran Gallery, Washington	
425	92	144	Lord Scarsdale	
426	52	143	National Gallery, London	
427	102		National Gallery, London	= HdG 448c
428			National Gallery, London	
429	262	90	National Gallery, London	= HdG 446
430	10	136	National Gallery, Washington	
431			Cologne sale 26 May 1971	
432	22	133	Buckingham Palace	
433	264	140	Marquess of Bute	
434	261		Dulwich College	
435	72	138	Dulwich College	
436	S28		Paris sale 1965	
436a	29		= HdG 61, 450	
437	91		Museum of Art, Raleigh	
438	120		= HdG 345	
440			London sale 8 Apr. 1970	
441			A. Pani, New York	
442			= HdG 8	
443			Paris sale 22 May 1929	
444	113		= HdG 337	
446	262		= HdG 429	
448	11	135	Toledo	= HdG 615
448a	40		= HdG 420	
448c	102		= HdG 427	
449	186	153	De Rothschild, Paris	
450	29		= HdG 61, 436a	
452	194		Dr Wetzlar, Amsterdam (1952)	
454	20		= HdG 226	
457	S12	155	Nazi looted property, Munich 1947	
458	S35	139	Amsterdam Rijksmuseum	
458a		137	Waddesdon Manor (NT)	= HdG 711
459			London sale 20 May 1927	
461			London sale 28 May 1937	= HdG 467
462			W. P. Chrysler, New York	
463			?Wroclaw	
464	142		= HdG 204, 338	
465	27	46	Cleveland	confused provenance
466			Petworth (NT)	
467	83		= HdG 461	
470			Glasgow	
470b			The Hague, Mauritshuis	see HdG 465
472			London sale 9 Apr. 1937	
473	S32	23	Private collection, England	= HdG 473a
473a	9		= HdG 473	
475			Aschaffenburg	
476			Copenhagen	
477	105		Lady Douglas Pennant	
479			Paris sale 7 Dec. 1951	
484		123	Charles Hickox, New York	
488	244	116	Buckingham Palace	
489	204		Wallace Collection, London	
490	67		Louvre, Paris	
491	18		Louvre, Paris	

HdG	Smith	Reiss	Last known collection	Other notes	HdG	Smith	Reiss	Last known collection	Other notes
500	245		Buckingham Palace		547			National Gallery, London	
501	227		Duke of Sutherland		548			Duke of Bedford	
502	S19		Van Gelder, Uccle (1908)		549	112	113	Buckingham Palace	
504			Antwerp		550	241	114	Buckingham Palace	
505			Edinburgh		550a	S33		= HdG 510	
506	213		Zurich dealer 1967		551			Dulwich College	
507	229		London sale 31 Mar. 1922		552	S37		Wallace Collection, London	
508			Sir Edmund Bacon		553			Wallace Collection, London	? = HdG 579, 584
509	191		London sale 24 Jun. 1970						
510	S33		Geneva sale 1938	= HdG 550a	554			T. Humphrey Ward 1908	
511	66	117	Private collection, America	= HdG 527	555			Apsley House, London	
					557			= HdG 353	
512	211		Wallace Collection, London		558	267		Munich	
					560	210		Philadelphia	cf. HdG 582
513	17		Wallace Collection, London	= HdG 526	561			Van der Vorm, Rotterdam	
514			New York Metropolitan	= HdG 516	562			Berlin sale 26 Sep. 1930	
515	271		Paris dealer 1948		563	S1		Leningrad	cf. HdG 560
516			= HdG 514		564			Petworth (NT)	
517		115	Art trade, Holland, 1949		565	215		London sale 11 Mar. 1964	= HdG 585
518			Von Schnitzler, Cologne, 1931	= HdG 581a					
					573	217		London sale 7 Jun. 1967	
519	270		Lady Douglas Pennant	= HdG 539	577			Fievez sale 30 Apr. 1947	
520			Prague		579			? = HdG 553, 584	
521			Ham House		581a			Private collection, Cologne	
525			Sedelmeyer 1896	= 530b					
525a	148		Brussels sale 1946		582			London sale 25 Feb. 1966	cf. HdG 560
526	17		= HdG 513						
527	S13		= HdG 511		584			? = HdG 553, 579	
529	251		London sale 17 Feb. 1950		585	215		London sale 11 Mar. 1964	
530b			= HdG 525		589			Weyer sale Apr. 1906	
531	219		New York sale 14 Nov. 1951		590			Philadelphia	
					591	235		Delbeke, Antwerp, 1908	
531a			London sale 15 Oct. 1948		593			Paris sale 1 Jun. 1956	Compare HdG 597
532a			London sale 18 May 1917						
532b			London sale 18 May 1917		594			Kleinberger	
534	S38		Thurkow, Hague		595	163		= HdG 40	
539	270		= HdG 519		596			At Agnews, London, 1938	
542			National Gallery, London		597	160		Private collection, Scotland	Compare HdG 593
543			Cambridge, Fitzwilliam						
544			Cambridge, Fitzwilliam		600	160		= HdG 597	
546	131		London sale 4 Jul. 1924		600b			London sale 14 Oct. 1937	

HdG	Smith	Reiss	Last known collection	Other notes
601			Compare HdG 593, 597, 600	
602			Wroclaw	
604			Dulwich College	
605	28		Dulwich College	
608			Bloudoff sale 1924	
609a	230		Dordrecht (DRVK)	= HdG 621, 624
612	249		Brooklyn	= HdG 614
614	249		= HdG 612	
615	11		= HdG 448	
616	174		Private collection, America	
617	150		= HdG 85	
618	177	124	National Gallery, Washington	
621	230		= HdG 609a, 624	
623b			London sale 18 Jun. 1954	
624	230		= HdG 609a, 621	
624b			Buckingham Palace	
626	S36		Art trade, Paris, 1911	
627	155	122	Birmingham, Barber Institute	
629			Marquess of Lansdowne	
630			Marquess of Lansdowne	
631	193		= HdG 165	
633	(24)	100	Frick Collection, New York	see HdG 640
634		30	Leipzig	
636			= HdG 167c	
637	247	99	Buckingham Palace	
638		19	National Gallery, London	= HdG 667, 677
639	25	102	Wallace Collection, London	
640	24	96	Wallace Collection	see HdG 633
641	171	110	Private collection, London	
643	14	142	Louvre, Paris	= HdG 650
644	S6		Leningrad	
645	S2		Leningrad	
646	228		Petworth (NT)	
647	216		= HdG 31	
648			Speelman, London	= HdG 671
648a		28	Toledo	
648b	1	32	Private collection, London	= HdG 649
649	1		= HdG 648b	
650	14		= HdG 643	
650b			London sale 30 Apr. 1937	= HdG 659
650c		22	Assheton-Bennett	
652	2		Toronto	= HdG 665
653			London sale 30 Nov. 1973	= HdG 662
654	S46		London sale 22 May 1963	
656g			Schoen, New York, 1934	
658	89	107	Institut Neerlandais, Paris	
659	255		= HdG 650b	
659e	201	109	Baron de Rothschild, Paris, 1939	
661a		33	J. Johnson Collection, Philadelphia	
662			= HdG 635	
663a			W. Stoye, Oxford, 1947	= HdG 670
665	2			
667			= HdG 638, 677	
668			Detroit Art Institute	
670			= HdG 663a	
671			= HdG 648	
671a			London sale 2 Feb. 1945	
676			National Art Collections Trust, London	
677			= HdG 638, 667	
677b			Exhibited Amsterdam 1929	
679	97		Art trade, New York, 1960s	
682			Destroyed by fire 1945	
683		12	Destroyed by fire 1945	
687			= HdG 219	
688		13	Dordrecht	
689		18	Frankfurt	
690			Bredius Museum, The Hague	
691		9	London sale 5 Dec. 1969	
692			London sale 5 Dec. 1969	= HdG 714
694		42	Dulwich College	
695			Dulwich College	
696			Dulwich College	
697	77		= HdG 239	

HdG	Smith	Reiss	Last known collection	Other notes
699			= HdG 228b	
700			Munich	
701			Corcoran Gallery, Washington	
702			Art trade, New York, 1950s	
703		20	London sale 1974	
704			St. Louis, Missouri	
706		63	Lord Egremont, Petworth	
707		62	Van der Vorm, Rotterdam	
708		27	Buhrle Foundation, Zurich	
709	94		= HdG 259	
711			= HdG 458a	
712			Residenz-Galerie, Salzburg	
713	269		London sale 7 Dec. 1960	
714			= HdG 692	
715		8	Art trade, London, 1969	
718b			Glasgow	
719	15		Six collection, Amsterdam	
720	85	34	Cologne	= HdG 727
721			Sir Edmund Bacon	
723	71		Earl of Normanton	
724	172	77	Engraving (Duke of Westminster)	
725			Leningrad	
727	85		= HdG 720	
728			Art trade, Holland, 1923	
730	250	75	Mezzotint (1773)	
732			London sale 13 Jul. 1945	
733	161	112	Duke of Bedford	? = HdG 738, 739b
734			Dulwich College	
735	26	151	National Gallery, London	= HdG 739
736	42		San Francisco	= HdG 740a
737	19	111	Earl of Yarborough	
738	3		? = HdG 733, 739b	
739	26		= HdG 735	
739b			? = HdG 733, 738	
740	279		London sale 5 Nov. 1966	
740a	42		= HdG 736	
744	212		Berlin	
745			Innsbruck	
749c			J. Johnson, Philadelphia	
753			Brussels	
754		65	Stockholm	
755			New York sale 29 Apr. 1915	
757			Brussels sale 11 Oct. 1955	
758		66	Private collection, Paris (1950)	= HdG 763a
762	184		Zurich dealer 1957	
763a			= HdG 758	
767	152		Duschnitz, Vienna, circa 1920	
772			De Groot, Hague	
773	153		Duke of Bedford	
774			Berlin sale 27 Feb. 1917	
775	119		Royal Collection, Holland	
776			Bachstitz, The Hague	
779			Rotterdam	
791			Paris dealer 1920	
797			Doordrecht	
798			Sir Edmund Bacon	
799			Sir Edmund Bacon	
800			The Hague, Mauritshuis	
802			Paris dealer 1920	
803			Paris sale 18 May 1922	= HdG 812
805			Schloss, Paris, 1908	
807			Rotterdam	
808	266		Schleissheim	
809d			Amsterdam dealer 1961	
809f			London dealer 1970	
810			Baron Thyssen, Lugano	
812			= HdG 803	
813			London dealer 1955	
818	246		Buckingham Palace	
819			London sale 10 Apr. 1937	
821			Rotterdam	
822b			Glasgow	
826			Lennep-Backer, Heemstede	
829			Rotterdam	
830			Rotterdam	
836			Philadelphia	
837			Philadelphia	
839			E.ten Cate, Almelo, 1953	

Appendix D:

SLINGELAND SALE, 1785

The most famous Cuyp collection was that formed in Dordrecht during the eighteenth century by Johan van der Linden van Slingeland. It included 38 pictures attributed to Cuyp and these were sold in Dordrecht in 1785. The buyers were mainly French and Dutch; for some reason the English dealers were not present on this occasion. This perhaps explains why the prices were rather lower than those ruling in this country at about that time.

Twenty-nine of the pictures can still be traced and possibly two others. The seven missing works were probably of no impor-tance and it may only be for this reason that they have disappeared. Of the 29, ten can be accepted as authentic while the other nine-teen are questionable, some much more so than others. Although the genuine pictures on the whole fetched the highest prices, there can be no doubt that the relative valuations would be totally different if the pictures were to be put on the market today.

Eight of the pictures listed in the catalogue (numbers R 69, 70, 71, 72, 78, 84, 85 and 102) were already possessed by van Slinge-land in 1752, when they were seen by Gerard Hoet (*Catalogus of Naamlyst van Schildereyen* II p. 490); Hoet also saw three others attributed to Cuyp which appear to have been sold in the interim (HdG 759, 767 and a picture comparable to HdG 36a).

Sale no.	Price florins	Category of subject	HdG	Reiss	Last known location	Remarks
69	1725	River scene	36	106	Waddesdon Manor	Accepted
70	1825	River scene	28	104	Washington	Accepted
71	1920	Hunting scene	430	136	Washington	Accepted
72	2650	Hunting scene	448	135	Toledo	Accepted
73	712	Rough sea	643	142	Louvre	School piece
74	505	Moonlight	719		Six collection	School piece
75	401	Cattle piece	207		Wallace Collection	School piece
76	501	Equestrian	513		Wallace Collection	School piece
77	602	Equestrian	490		Louvre	School piece
78	1705	Winter scene	737	111	Earl of Yarborough	Accepted
79	530	Horse fair	40	150	Rikoff sale 1907	School piece
80	1555	Rhineland	226	152	Private Collection	School piece
81	1007	Milking scene	367		Art trade 1956	Doubtful
82	1250	Rhineland	432	133	Buckingham Palace	Accepted
83	172	Equestrian	495			Missing
84	1300	River scene	639	102	Wallace Collection	Accepted
85	850	River scene	633	100	Frick Collection	Accepted
86	190	Winter scene	739	151	National Gallery	School piece
87	577	Italianate	465	46	Cleveland	Accepted
88	470	Riding school	605		Dulwich College	School piece
89	110	Equestrian	61		New York sale 1922	School piece
90	59	River scene	650a			Missing
91	97	River scene	650b		Loyd sale 1937	Doubtful
92	40	Van Goyenesque	650c	22	Assheton-Bennett	Accepted
93	13	Van Goyenesque	682		Burnt 1945 (Berlin)	Doubtful
94	405	Historical	27	148	Vienna sale 1933	School piece
95	237	Cattle dealer	39		London sale 1969	School piece
96	245	Cattle scene	191		Lille Museum	Identification uncertain
97	350	Milking scene	380a			Missing
98	91	Battle scene	57		Amsterdam	School piece
99	105	Rhineland	398	39	DRVK, Hague	Identification uncertain
100	377	Rhineland	418		Thyssen, Lugano	Doubtful
101	325	Religious	10		Dr Wetzlar	Doubtful
102	36	Moonlight	725c			Missing
103	305	Cattle scene	341		Marquis d'Aoust, 1908	Doubtful
104	146	Seaport	651			Missing
105	166	Moonlight	726			Missing
106	50	Genre	148a			Missing

Appendix E :

A NOTE ON CUYP'S IMITATORS

Although the records are completely silent on the subject, there is little doubt that Cuyp's style was being imitated from a comparatively early date. In no other way is it possible to explain the existence of so many pictures which though bearing the typical Cuyp insignia and plainly belonging to the 1640s and 1650s, yet do not possess sufficient quality to justify the name given to them. Moreover, it is reasonable to assume that the highly gifted son of a well-known father – Jacob Gerritsz Cuyp had long been Dordrecht's leading painter – would not have been entirely overlooked by his contemporaries.

The fact that none of Cuyp's early imitators succeeded in establishing an independent reputation suggests that the standard of his following was comparatively low. Was this merely a matter of chance, or was there some specific reason which tended to discourage the more talented students from entering his studio? The latter hypothesis cannot be ruled out. It is perhaps relevant that,

in 1642, Jacob Gerritsz Cuyp and a few of his colleagues broke away from the Guild of the Five Trades and set up their own independent Painters' Guild. As the records of the period have been lost, the precise reasons for their action cannot be determined. It is quite possible, however, that they wished to introduce and enforce regulations – not uncommon at the time – which effectively prevented an ex-pupil from setting up in open competition with his former master.

If this supposition were to prove correct, it would explain not only the fact that the name of Cuyp appears firmly imprinted on so many pictures of inferior quality but also the departure from the town at an early age of several of Dordrecht's most gifted painters, such as Maes, Hoogstraeten and Levecq. It seems that for a period of about fifteen years, the two Cuyps held a virtual monopoly of portrait and landscape painting in Dordrecht, and that it was not until Maes returned in the mid 1650s that this monopoly was gradually broken.

Although the names of a few of the elder Cuyp's followers are known, they were mostly portrait painters of an earlier generation

Cornelis Tegelberg, the author of this landscape (on panel 35.5 x 63 cm, collection H. Trojanski, Dusseldorf), was one of the founders of the Dordrecht Painters' Guild in 1642. Only one other painting by his hand is at present recognized. Both pictures show the influence of Jacob Gerritsz rather than Aelbert Cuyp. It is possible, however, that Tegelberg later adopted the style of the younger master.

than Aelbert. Houbraken does, however, mention the name of one animal painter who was a younger man than Aelbert: Bastian Govertsz van der Leeuw (1624–1680). This artist was registered as an apprentice in 1638 and subsequently had two sons who were also painters. According to Houbraken he later gave up painting and kept a tavern.

No painting by this artist can at present be identified. Being three and a half years younger than Aelbert, it is reasonable to assume that it was Aelbert's rather than Jacob's style that he followed. Possibly he remained Aelbert's assistant and close imitator throughout both their painting careers. No doubt, also, he passed on the master's style to his two sons: Gabriel (1645–1688) and Pieter (1647–1679); before long they radically changed direction but perhaps not until they too had contributed substantially to the oeuvre traditionally ascribed to Cuyp.

Mention has already been made of the two van Calraet brothers: Abraham (1642–1722) and Barent (1649–1737). They were exact contemporaries of the younger van der Leeuws and belong essentially to the period when the standard of Dutch painting was declining rapidly. Their importance has been greatly exaggerated. Much closer to Cuyp must have been those painters – their names are at present largely unknown – who were more nearly his contemporaries.

Until many years later, Cuyp's influence did not spread beyond Dordrecht. While he remained comparatively unknown, there was no reason to attach his name to pictures with which he had no direct connection. When, however, during the second half of the 18th century, the demand for his work began to grow, similarities were found in many paintings of his time and his alleged oeuvre was steadily increased by spurious means.

To list all the painters who have at some stage been confused with Cuyp would be impossible. However, the following classification may be useful in indicating the main areas where confusion has arisen. If no painting by the artist can at present be identified, the name is given in italics.

1. Painters associated with Jacob Gerritsz Cuyp (1594–1651/2): Dirk van Hoogstraeten (1595–1640), Simon Peter Tilemann (1601–c. 69), Cornelis Tegelberg (dates unknown), *Izaak van Hasselt* (dates unknown), J. F. van der Merck (c. 1610–64), Jan Olis (c. 1610–76), Paulus Lesire (1611–after 1650), Benjamin Cuyp (1612–52), *Bastian van der Leeuw* (1624–80).

2. Painters associated with Jan van Goyen (1596–1656): Francois Knipbergen (1597–c. 1665), A. J. van der Croos (c. 1606–c. 62), F. de Hulst (c. 1610–61), P. Nolpe (1613/4–1652/3), Joost Vinck (dates unknown), Johannes Ruysscher (c. 1625–c. 75).

3. Painters associated with Simon de Vlieger (c. 1600–53): Hendrik de Meyer (c. 1620–83), Lieve Verschuier (c. 1630–86).

4. Painters associated with Jan Both (c. 1614–52): *Barend Bisbinck* (c. 1630–c. 57), Willem van Drielenburg (1632–after 1677) and probably others.

5. Painters associated with Paulus Potter (1625–54): Albert Klomp (1618–79), Hendrik Mommers (1623–93), Anthonie van Borssum (1629/30–77).

6. Painters associated with Dirk Stoop (c. 1618–86): Ludolf de Jongh (1616–79), A. C. Beeldemaeker (c. 1625–after 1701).

7. Dordrecht painters who may have been pupils of Aelbert Cuyp (1620–91): Hubertus Ravesteyn (1638–c. 1688), Abraham van Calraet (1642–1722), Gabriel van der Leeuw (1645–88), Pieter van der Leeuw (1647–79), Barent van Calraet (1649–1737).

In considering the painters of a later period, attention has always been drawn first and foremost to the two van Strijs, Abraham (1753–1826) and Jacob (1756–1815). It might be supposed that, by now, their ability to deceive had been completely exhausted. As the van Gelders have recently shown, however, this is very far from so (*Nederlands Kunsthistorisch Jaarboek* 1972 p. 231). Equally, it would also be a mistake to imagine that the van Strijs were the only painters of the late eighteenth century capable of successful deception. By 1780, England was the centre of the Cuyp market and many highly skilled painters had links with the London art trade, among them Julius Caesar Ibbetson (1759–1817). In the Chauncey sale of 26 March 1790 a picture is listed as: 'CUYP – a group of cattle, by Ibbetson, after.' It would be interesting to know what has become of this picture and the many others like it. The quality can hardly have been negligible.

BIBLIOGRAPHY

Seventeenth Century Dordrecht
M. BALEN, *Beschryvinge der Stad Dordrecht*, 1677.

Biographical
A. HOUBRAKEN, *De Groote Schouburgh der Nederlantsche Konstschilders en Schilder-essen*, 1718–21 (see page 198).

J. H. VETH, *Oud Holland*, 1884 page 243ff, page 270ff, and 1888 page 143ff.

E. MICHEL, *Gazette des Beaux-Arts*, 1892 page 107ff and 225ff.

Works
W. BUCHANAN, *The Memoirs of Painting*, 1824.

J. SMITH, *A Catalogue Raisonné of the Works of the Most Eminent Dutch, Flemish and French Painters*, volume V, 1834 (with supplement 1842), *see* page 200.

G. F. WAAGEN, *The Treasures of Art in Great Britain*, 1854 (supplement 1857).

H. DE GROOT, *A Catalogue Raisonné of the Works of the Most Eminent Dutch Painters of the Seventeenth Century*, volume II, English edition 1909, *see* page 204.

There is also much further information concerning the history of the pictures to be obtained by research into the readily available sale catalogues of the eighteenth century (see F. Simpson, *Burlington Magazine*, February 1953 page 39ff).

Artistic development
W. STECHOW, 'Significant Dates on Some Seventeenth Century Landscape Paintings', *Oud Holland* 1960 page 79ff.
Dutch Landscape Painting of the Seventeenth Century, 1966.

H. GERSON, 'Aelbert Cuyp's gezicht van het Wachthuis in de Kil', *Opus musivum, Feestbundel voor Prof. Dr M. D. Ozinga*, 1964 page 257ff.

G. DUITS, *Duits Quarterly*, volume XII, 1968.

J. G. VAN GELDER AND INGRID JOST, 'Vroeg contact van Aelbert Cuyp met Utrecht', *Miscellanea I.Q. van Regteren Altena*, 1969 page 100ff.
'Doorzagen op Aelbert Cuyp', *Nederlands Kunsthistorisch Jaarboek* 1972 page 223ff.

Associated painters
ULRICH THIEME AND FELIX BECKER, *Allgemeines Lexikon der Bildenden Künstler* volume XIX, 1926, page 482ff (article on A. van Kalraet by Hofstede de Groot).

J. NIEUWSTRATEN, 'De ontwikkeling van Herman Saftleven's kunst tot 1650', *Nederlands Kunsthistorisch Jaarboek* 1965, page 81ff.

General
M. BRYAN, *A Dictionary of Painters*, 1816.

E. FROMENTIN, *Les Maîtres d'autrefois*, 1876 (English edition introduced by H. Gerson 1948).

W. BODE, *Rembrandt und seine Zeitgenossen*, 1907 (English edition 1909: 'Great Masters of Dutch and Flemish Painting').

J. A. CROWE, *Encyclopaedia Britannica*, Eleventh Edition, 1910, volume VII page 677ff.

A. VON WURZBACH, *Niederländisches Künstler-Lexikon*, 1906-11.

Dordrecht circa 1640

This map, published by Blaeu, shows Dordrecht more or less
as it was at the time that Cuyp painted his early panoramic view
of the town in the mid 1640s (R29/30). Major changes to the
waterfront were begun in 1647 and these are incorporated in the
map opposite, although neither map can be accepted as entirely
accurate.

The principal landmarks are the Great Church on the left, the
Groothoofdspoort slightly right of centre (with the cluster of
boats in front), and the Rietdijkspoort on the extreme right of
the town. The map is set approximately northwest.

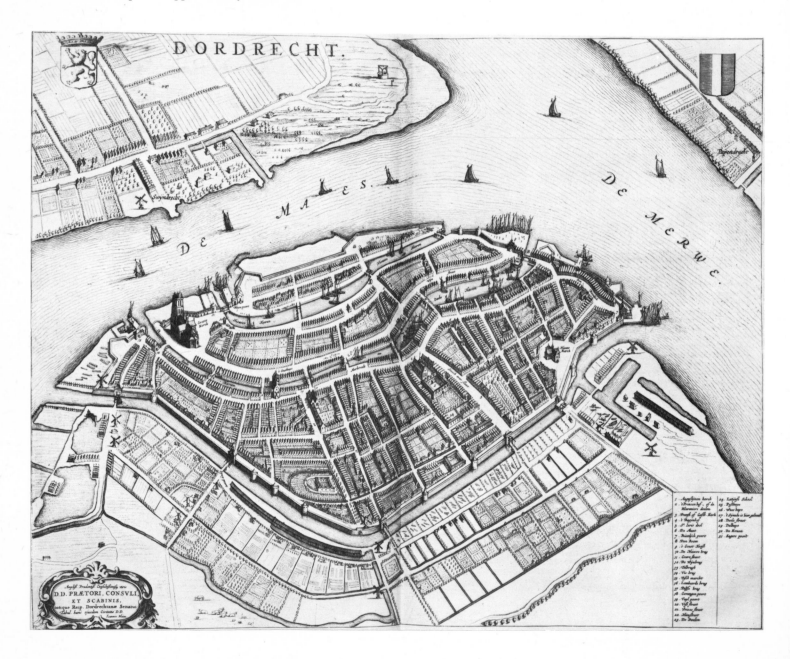

Dordrecht circa 1675

Also set approximately northwest, this map appears in Matthys Balen's *Beschryvinge der Stad Dordrecht*, 1677. When compared with the Blaeu map opposite, several differences may be noticed, for instance new harbours have been constructed at both extremities of the town and another immediately in front of the Great Church. The central frontage has also been extended beyond the old ramparts of the town. Incidentally, there was no consistency then – as now – in the naming of the river. Maas (or Maes) and Merwede (or Merwe) appear to have been interchangeable, though the division shown on the Blaeu map is probably supported by the greatest weight of tradition.

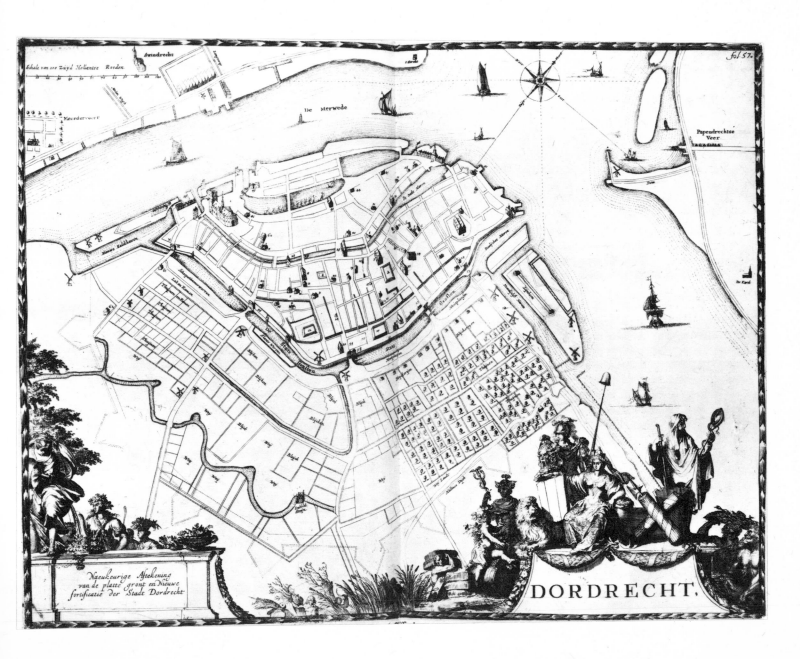

ACKNOWLEDGEMENTS

A book of this nature depends on the help of many people, in particular the owners of the pictures. Most owners have responded generously; only a few have failed to reply or declined to cooperate. The questioning of long established beliefs is bound to arouse suspicion. Happily, however, the damage has not been serious and it has proved possible to include some visual record, if not always the best, of every picture considered essential for an understanding of Cuyp's stylistic development. Special thanks are due to the staffs of the Witt Library, London, and of the Rijksbureau voor Kunsthistorische Documentatie at The Hague, to Professors Sir Ellis Waterhouse and J. G. van Gelder for valuable advice on certain points, and to Maurice Ash for his decisive encouragement.

Corrections and additions

R6 (page 32): this picture is on canvas not panel.

R72 (page 109): this picture, which was exhibited at Agnew's in June 1975, has benefitted greatly from cleaning. This has revealed that it was originally painted as an oval, a feature unique in Cuyp's oeuvre as far as we know.

R89 (page 126): an exact watercolour copy of this picture by Jacob van Strij was exhibited at Dordrecht in 1956. This does not help to dispel any lurking doubts about the painting.

R147 (page 191): this small panel, evidently the work of an early Cuyp scholar, has been discovered in the collection of the Earl and Countess of Swinton, Masham, Yorkshire.

Page 206: HdG 272b was sold at Christies on 14 February 1975.

Page 208: HdG 412 was sold at Christies on 27 June 1975.

Page 214 (list 2): Dr Gerson has argued forcibly (Nederlands Kunsthistorisch Jaarboek 1947 page 95ff.) that every painting attributed to Pieter Nolpe is in fact the work of Pieter de Neijn (1597-1639). This theory may be undermined, however, by the existence of a winter scene, formerly in the Mayer collection, which was sold by Graupe on 25 June 1934. This bears the PN monogram and is dated 1642. It is the painter of this picture, whatever his name, who has sometimes been confused with Cuyp.

INDEX